Advance Praise for *Guided*

"On a personal note, in 2004, Hans shared a vision he had that 'a soul is calling and wants me to be his father.' My wife and I had not even spoken about adoption, but lo and behold, an infant boy was given to us weeks later. Jared is our son and I have no clue what life would be like without his amazing heart and soul being a part of this family. He is divine and pure love. We are grateful to Hans King for eternity."

—Craig Shoemaker, host of *The Craig Shoemaker Show*, winner of the prestigious Communicator Award

"Hans Christian King's heart of gold shines through these pages as a window to the soul. His integrity, maturity, and dedication to service are impeccable. *Guided* contains countless gems of wisdom based on his five decades of experience as a medium. I was touched, enlightened, and inspired. My respect for Hans's work is immense. This book is a must-read for anyone seeking to explore the realm of mediumship and psychic guidance."

—Alan Cohen, author of *A Course in Miracles Made Easy*

"Hans teaches us how to dig deep within our souls to find ourselves. I love the message."

—George Noory, host of *Coast to Coast AM*

"True wisdom can only come from having distilled spiritual truths from a life lived with awareness, mindfulness, and love. Hans Christian King has lived such a life. Now, in his new book, *Guided*, he offers us gems of wisdom that inspire us to put our best foot forward in our journey of awakening to the light and grace of Spirit. In his inimitable manner, sculpted by five decades of devotion to healing and teaching thousands of souls, Hans compassionately guides us, step-by-step, in how to live a truly spirit-centered life."

—Michael J. Tamura, spiritual teacher, clairvoyant visionary, and author of *You Are the Answer*

"How can we connect with our intuitive guidance and recognize it? This book is an enormously useful and clear guide to understanding and cooperating with our natural abilities and connecting with our true nature as spiritual beings. Wise and inspiring, full of experiences and suggestions for practice, I recommend it to all those wanting to understand and learn about their true nature."

—Ellen Miller, spiritual teacher and co-author of *Silence and the Soul: Awakening Inner Wisdom*

"Hans King invites the reader into the remarkable world of mediumship. He shares with us what it is like to walk in two worlds, the everyday life we all share and the unseen life of spirit that informs and guides us on our way. . . . I highly recommend this book to anyone seeking to connect with their own inner wisdom and to begin a most profound relationship, one that will change their life and bring grace to their everyday experience."

—Gary Sherman, author of *Perceptual Integration: The Mechanics of Awakening* and co-author of *Silence and the Soul: Awakening Inner Wisdom*

"*Guided* is a profound look into the world of mediumship through the eyes of an experienced and deeply compassionate medium. Hans King shares the kinds of personal experiences that can only come from decades of walking with Spirit and providing comfort and guidance to thousands of people. In *Guided*, Hans shares practical guidance on how you can learn to uncover your own intuitive abilities. I have had the honor of working with many healers, mediums, and spiritual teachers, and what makes Hans's gifts so remarkable and different from the rest is that he truly comes from a place of authentic service to mankind. I highly recommend not only his books but his work."

—Daniel Gutierrez, bestselling author, global speaker, world trans-
formational leader, master business/life coach, and philosopher

"*Guided* is an incredible book filled with guidance, answers, and love. It is one of those rare books that opens the door to questions that many of us internally ask but don't know how to verbalize. Hans Christian King shares the answers, and through his masterful writing expands awareness. Read *Guided* and be prepared to feel love and come to know the majesty of yourself and your journey with greater clarity as you awaken your intuitive voice of your soul."

—Chuck Gallagher, business ethics expert, consultant,
keynote speaker, and author of *Second Chances:
Transforming Adversity into Opportunity*

Guided

RECLAIMING THE INTUITIVE
VOICE OF YOUR SOUL

Hans Christian King

ATRIA
—
ENLIVEN BOOKS
NEW YORK   TORONTO   LONDON   SYDNEY   NEW DELHI

ATRIA BOOKS

ENLIVEN

Enliven Books
An Imprint of Simon & Schuster, Inc.
1230 Avenue of the Americas
New York, NY 10020

First Enliven Books hardcover edition November 2016

This publication contains the opinions and ideas of its author. It is intended to provide helpful and informative material on the subjects addressed in the publication. It is sold with the understanding that the author and publisher are not engaged in rendering medical, health, or any other kind of personal professional services in the book. The reader should consult his or her medical, health, or other competent professional before adopting any of the suggestions in this book or drawing inferences from it.

The author and publisher specifically disclaim all responsibility for any liability, loss, or risk, personal or otherwise, which is incurred as a consequence, directly or indirectly, of the use and application of any of the contents of this book.

ATRIA BOOKS / ENLIVEN and colophons are trademarks of Simon & Schuster, Inc.

For information about special discounts for bulk purchases, please contact Simon & Schuster Special Sales at 1-866-506-1949 or business@simonandschuster.com.

The Simon & Schuster Speakers Bureau can bring authors to your live event. For more information or to book an event, contact the Simon & Schuster Speakers Bureau at 1-866-248-3049 or visit our website at www.simonspeakers.com.

Interior design by Kyoko Watanabe

Manufactured in the United States of America

10 9 8 7 6 5 4 3 2 1

Library of Congress Cataloging-in-Publication Data

Names: King, Hans Christian, author.
Title: Guided : reclaiming the intuitive voice of your soul / by Hans Christian King.
Description: First Edition. | New York : Enliven Books, 2016. | Includes bibliographical references.
Identifiers: LCCN 2016012647 | ISBN 9781501129094 (hardcover)
Subjects: LCSH: Psychic ability. | Spiritual life. | Spiritualism. | Guides (Spiritualism)
Classification: LCC BF1031 .K495 2016 | DDC 133.9—dc23
LC record available at https://lccn.loc.gov/2016012647

ISBN 978-1-5011-2909-4
ISBN 978-1-5011-2912-4 (ebook)

I lovingly dedicate this book to my father,
H. Douglas King, who unconditionally supported
me and was my rock throughout his lifetime.

CONTENTS

x CONTENTS

Foreword

"USE THE LIGHT that dwells within you to regain your natural clarity of sight," Lao-Tzu wisely instructs us. The book you hold in your hands is a personal introduction to that light, the greatest clarifier among your innate gifts: *intuition*. Throughout his more than fifty years of mediumship and teaching, Hans King has enabled countless clients and students to remove the obstacles that block, hinder, or sabotage the light of clear-sightedness, allowing them to make the highest use of what he calls the "intuitive intelligence of the heart," otherwise known as clairsentience or intuition.

With profound wisdom and compassion this book addresses some of the most fundamental questions of existence we human beings have been asking since time immemorial. Who am I? Why am I here? Where will I go when I leave the three-dimensional world? Will I meet my departed loved ones there? Are they still connected to me in such a way that we can communicate from our separate universes? Why do I feel that they are sometimes present in an assisting, guiding way? And do I feel like I've lived before because I actually have?

On the spiritual path we speak of the individual soul having continuity of consciousness beyond our three-dimensional existence, and of inexplicable mysteries, including the finite nature of our world and the infinite realms that emerge from an ineffable Creator Source. Such explorations are not initiated in the human mind, because it is incapable of wrapping itself around the workings of eternity. Rather, they arise when we strike a mystic chord of memory within our spirit-soul, reminding us of our cosmic origin. The work and teachings of Hans King transmit to us the ways in which we can consciously strike that chord, especially when we most need its grace-filled guidance.

When I first met Hans, in 2005, I immediately knew I was in the presence of an individual who walked in two worlds—one with earthly sure-footedness, and one with otherworldly transcendence. Recognizing his humility, compassionate heart, integrity, and professionalism, I was moved to invite him into the spiritual organization I founded, the Agape International Spiritual Center, where he has been a featured speaker at our annual conference, given classes in our university, and conducted reading sessions with many individuals within the Agape community.

As a father and grandfather, I am especially moved by Hans's wise counsel—which is described in detail in this book—about the ways in which parents can support their children in identifying the purpose for which they have come on the planet, and supporting them in fulfilling it. With profound and practical wisdom he teaches us how to prevent societal conditioning from robbing our children of living the unique expression of spirit that they are. For that reason alone I have recommended this book to both new and seasoned parents—grandparents as well—because it's never too late for resurrecting a child's soul-memory of his or her life path.

Guided is an extension of Hans's immeasurable connection to the spirit world and his dharmic calling to teach and counsel those whom spirit directs to him. Writing with great warmth, sensitivity, and clarity, Hans brings his teachings, mediumship, and work with clients alive through personal stories, case histories, and inner practices that will illuminate and bless the lives they touch. I recommend keeping this liberating book near at hand, and reading it again and again.

—MICHAEL BERNARD BECKWITH,
AUTHOR OF *SPIRITUAL LIBERATION* AND *LIFE VISIONING*

A Note to the Reader

IT IS MY hope that by writing this book and sharing my life's work as a medium and teacher, I can help guide you to your authenticity and purpose. I know from my fifty plus years of experience, seeing the evidence firsthand, that there is no separation between spirits and humans; and it's possible for anyone to communicate with them. By doing so, we can receive invaluable information that demystifies and clarifies many aspects of our lives—answers to the perennial questions "Who am I?" and "Why am I here?"

We are all more than what meets the eye, and how we sense, feel, and relate to the world within and around us is pivotal to sculpting our life according to its highest design. Attuning our inner ear and inner eye to the spirit world creates a reality that is far richer and enriching than you could ever imagine, and yet it is accessible to us. I will go further to say that our intuition is the voice of spirit itself, connecting each of us to a world of loving and wise spirit guides. Our part is to become open and receptive to such grace-filled generosity and demonstrate our gratitude by using this guiding compass in all aspects of our life.

So whether you were drawn to this book in order to deepen your understanding of your intuitive faculties, the realities of the three-dimensional realm and those beyond, the continuity of individual consciousness after physical death, or our unbroken connection to the spirit world and our departed loved ones, the content of this book reflects my heart's utmost intention to provide a precious vehicle that puts your own heart at peace and accelerates your soul's evolutionary progress.

How to Best Use This Book

Ervin Laszlo, founder of systems philosophy and evolution theory, received the highest degree in human sciences from the Sorbonne and was twice nominated for the Nobel Peace Prize. In his book *The Immortal Mind*—which includes a detailed history of scientific studies on medium-transmitted communication, past life recollection, reincarnation, and the Akasha—he writes, "A credible explanation of how consciousness could persist beyond the brain would overcome both the skeptical and the religious preconceptions. Many more apparitions, visions, and instances of after-death communication would be experienced by ordinary people and reported without fear of ridicule and without recourse to religious doctrine."[1]

The client stories described in this book are supported by Mr. Laszlo's scientific findings that as more individuals experience their connection to the spirit world, the collective paradigm also shifts, resulting in people feeling "normal" as they intuitively communicate with spirit, guides, and their departed loved ones. Certainly one of the most tender experiences I cherish in my work with clients is that moment when they directly experience how their departed loved ones yearn to reach out to them, resolve unfinished business, share new insights, and honor agreements which were made while they shared living on the Earth plane, on the other side, or both.

Guided is organized into twelve chapters, each one focusing on a spiritual principle that will guide, inspire, and encourage you to reactivate your innate intuitive power of clairsentience. The chapters naturally build upon each other, like a journey that progresses each step of the way. I recommend you experience the book in this manner, and take along a journal to capture your thoughts and insights. Of course, if there is a particular chapter that resonates with you and you wish to skip ahead, then please trust this feeling—there could be a reason why it's calling out to you. And then, you can always come back to the other chapters.

The Bringing It All Home practices at the end of each chapter have been designed with one expert in mind who, for however many years he or she has been gracing the planet, has accumulated the life experience required to benefit from them. That expert guide is *you*, dear reader. And so it is that I thank you for your presence on this side of existence and your willingness to open your heart to the other side and receive the wealth of blessings that await you. It is then that you will come to appreciate James Allen's words: "They themselves are makers of themselves," for indeed, you co-create your life with spirit and all those who so profoundly love you—seen and unseen.

I invite you to be curious, courageous, and creative in your use of this book. May it open for you the doors of limitless perception, both on this and on the other side of the veil. And I thank you for allowing me to share what I've learned from over fifty years of walking this life as a medium and intuitive teacher, bridging the gap between our earthly and spiritual worlds.

—HANS C. KING, 2016

Guided

✳

CHAPTER 1

Heaven's Language

I HAVE FOUND real proof of life after death. What I share in this book is based on the reality of my personal life's experience, and my fifty plus years of work as a medium and teacher for thousands of clients. I was born clairsentient, clairvoyant, and clairaudient. Of course, when these abilities came into expression at the age of three I had no definitions for them, nor was I aware that those in my immediate surroundings did not experience these same innate aspects of their being. But not for long, thanks to my master guide, Sebastian, who first introduced himself to me at that time.

During my formative years, my spirit guides would talk with me and take me on what I related to as *Alice's Adventures in Wonderland*–type excursions where I would be in a room which all of a sudden grew very, very large while I became very tiny among individuals who were never under seven feet tall. (I never questioned why there was this discrepancy in height as I was totally immersed and delighted in the experience itself.) This out-of-body travel in my astral form, captained by Sebastian, went on for several years. Eventually, I grew to understand that one of the foremost teachings my guides were transmitting to me was the importance of seeing through illusory appearances, to see with the eye of the soul the subtlety behind the façade of the obvious. To illustrate, the following story describes one of the early childhood voyages my guides and I embarked upon together.

While quietly playing in my parents' home, a group of my guides—around three of them, led by Sebastian—entered my bedroom and, in my astral body, ushered me into the backyard. We stopped before a tree where a caterpillar was peacefully chomping on a leaf. At the time, I assumed we were simply enjoying and observing one of the beauties of nature at work.

Then, when a couple of days later we journeyed outside the room to the same tree, the caterpillar was beginning to build its cocoon. Turning to me one of my guides asked, "And what do you see, son?" to which I responded, "I see the caterpillar playing with some white stuff."

"Are you sure that's what you see?" he again asked, with heavy emphasis on the word "sure," at which point I wordlessly answered by raising my eyebrows and widening my eyes.

When during our next visit the caterpillar disappeared into its cocoon, the question became, "And now what do you see, Hans?" I responded with the obvious, "I see the caterpillar's cocoon."

"So where is the caterpillar?" another guide queried and to which I replied, "Well, I guess it's in the cocoon, but I can't see through it so I don't know for sure."

Our final pilgrimage to the tree was just in time for me to witness a butterfly—a black and yellow Monarch—majestically emerge from the cocoon. Alarmed, I asked, "It's beautiful, but what happened to the little caterpillar?"

Most tenderly Sebastian leaned toward me and said, "Learn from this, son, that in the human realm things are not always as they appear. You must always make yourself available to the miracles in life by not mistaking for reality what your outer eyes and ears tell you. Learn to listen with the inner ear and see with the inner eye of your soul, then the truths of existence will become transparent to you."

When I returned to my room, I phonetically sounded out the word "transparent" and looked it up in the dictionary. I share it with you here as defined in *Webster's Universal College Dictionary*: "Having the property of transmitting rays of light through its substance so that bodies situated beyond or behind can be distinctly seen." Although some of this vocabulary exceeded my understanding, I intuitively grasped that through the caterpillar-butterfly transformation, my guides were giving me an object lesson: It is with the inner light of the soul's eye that we see through the density of outer appearances to the truth of their essential essence. This universal principle remained with me, and as I grew up I came to call it "attuning to the voice in your soul." In other words: *intuition*.

Beginning at around the age of six, I became aware of the fact that I was different from other children—not only because they treated me differently than they did other classmates or playmates, but due to the simple fact that I *was* different. Not in any "special" way, nor in a way for which I had words. It was something they sensed, and for which they also lacked words, which caused them to shy away from me. So when I felt left out of their games or events I turned to Sebastian, asking him if there was something I needed to do so they would include me. "You must learn to walk in both worlds," he instructed me, "the world you see with your physical eyes, and the world you see with the inner eye of your spirit, which is the same eye with which you see me and others in the spirit world."

His loving kindness got me through not only grade school and middle school, it also supported me when, in my junior year of high school, with parental permission I chose to broaden my horizons by enlisting as a yeoman in the United States Navy. It's then that I discovered there are no geographical healings, that wherever you go, there you are. Even out at sea sailors older than myself would seek me out to confide their personal struggles and ask for advice, saying they trusted what they sensed to be something "different" about me. Although I didn't share that my guidance to them was from the spirit world, the fact that they saw my being different as something that contributed to their lives deeply touched my heart.

As for my Navy career, I told myself that I'd picked this profession by proxy, since I'd always wanted to be a fireman when I grew up. However, when I completed my tour of duty and was honorably discharged from the Navy at the age of nineteen, I realized I wasn't too far off, the only difference being that rather than extinguishing outer fires, I was putting out the inner fires of self-doubt, fear, anger, and the anguish of loss in the hearts of those who sought me out.

Upon leaving the Navy and following spiritual guidance that this was my true calling in life, I began formally seeing clients and creating a private practice. Thus began my formal entry into the profession of mediumship, and fifty-five years later, it is what I continue to do with passion.

Sebastian, my treasured master guide, has faithfully been at my side from the age of three to this day, guiding me through my life journey and purpose. I pray that I have been as faithful a student to him as he has been a master guide, teacher, and friend to me. He has fanned the flames of my passionate commitment to my purpose as a direct-voice medium, to using heaven's language to support all those who cross my path in connecting to their true Self, to realize they never have been nor ever shall be separate from spirit nor their loved ones. The dedication underlying my work is to establish this reconnection by providing substantive, factual evidence that it is possible to communicate with our loved ones on the other side and receive invaluable information from them that demystifies and clarifies aspects of one's life.

My readings for thousands of individuals across the spectrum of cultures, ethnicities, economic levels, religious beliefs, and spiritual practices reveal the universal human yearning to receive an answer to the perennial questions of our existence: "Who am I?," "Why am I here?," and "Where will I go when I'm no longer here?"

Our Birthright: Intuition

For most of us, the search for the truths of existence in general and ours in particular has been anything but clear and simple; rather, it is frequently blurred and confusing. And it's no surprise, for when we come into this world society provides us with a map describing the acceptable borders of beliefs, concepts, morals, experiences, and religious dogmas in which we are expected to contain ourselves. All of this unavoidable societal conditioning causes us to live in such a way that takes us further away from rather than closer to our authentic self, to a conscious connection to the vastness of our true nature and our purpose for having taken a human incarnation. One of the main purposes of this book is to support its readers in breaking through the borders of the societal myths and conditioning and reclaim one of our most valuable innate gifts, intuition.

I feel it is important to clarify that although women are stereotyped as being intuitive and men as being insensitive, this is a great inaccuracy. *All beings are equipped with their birthright of intuition.* To the gentlemen reading this book, this means you are now free to step out of your intuitive closet and fully claim this faculty that accompanied you in your birth suitcase. The determining factor for accepting and activating intuition, I believe, is to be found in the different social conditioning men and women receive during their upbringing, education, religion, and cultural mores. In case you are one of those fortunate men or women who, in spite of conditioning, bravely fired up your self-reliance, tossed society's faulty map over a cliff, and embarked on your own unique journey, together we will create a new map that will lead you into even deeper recesses of consciousness.

Activating the Intuitive Voice: Clairsentience

Did you know that you apply intuition on a daily basis? In everyday language we call it a hunch, gut instinct, a vibe, an "I feel it in my bones" awareness. In the field of parapsychology, *clairsentience*—or psychic and intuitive ability—is considered a form of extrasensory perception wherein a person has the ability to feel and experience the energy in an intuitive way; this stream of energy offers psychic guidance through vivid feeling or insights. The word *clair* is French for "clear," and "sentience" is derived from the Latin *sentire*, which means "to feel."

Clairsentience is a direct, clear feeling without tangible evidence provided by the five senses. Many of the world's wisdom traditions refer to it as a sixth sense, which the *Oxford English Dictionary* defines as "A supposed intuitive faculty by which a person or animal perceives facts and regulates action without the direct use of any of the five senses."

Soon after his reelection on November 10, 1864, President Abraham Lincoln confided to his close friend and bodyguard, Ward Hill Lamon, a clairsentient dream he had had of his own body lying in state in the White House. "Who is dead in the White House?" the dreaming Lincoln asked a soldier standing guard. "The President. He was killed by an assassin."

On the evening of April 14, 1865, while attending a performance of the comedy *Our American Cousin*, Lincoln was assassinated by the famous stage actor and Confederate sympathizer John Wilkes Booth. At 7:22 AM the next day, Lincoln died. His body lay in state on April 18, just five months after his dream.

The belief in clairsentience dates back thousands of years. The Greek historian Herodotus wrote that Croesus, who in the sixth century BC ruled what is now Turkey, consulted oracles. An oracle is someone who offers advice or a prophecy that is considered to be directly channeled from a Divine Source. Then in 399 BC, in his *Apology*, Plato claims that the oracle at Delphi played a vital role in the life of the philosopher Socrates.

His Holiness the Dalai Lama describes in his 1990 autobiography, *Freedom in Exile*, how he, too, seeks guidance from an oracle. In the Tibetan Buddhist tradition, an oracle is a powerful spirit channeled by a human medium. The Venerable Thupten Ngodup was officially enthroned in 1988 as the Nechung Medium, the Chief State Oracle of Tibet. About him the Dalai Lama wrote:

> For hundreds of years now, it has been traditional for the Dalai Lama to consult the Nechung Medium during the New Year Festivals. I myself have dealings with him [Thupten Ngodup] several times a year. This may sound far-fetched to twentieth-century Western readers. Even some Tibetans, mostly those who consider themselves "progressive," have misgivings about my continued use of this ancient method of intelligence gathering. But I do so for the simple reason that as I look back over the many occasions when I have asked questions of the oracle, on each one of them time has proved that his answer was correct.[1]

Clairsentience also functions in situations as simple as deciding, for no apparent reason, to take a different route to work and later hear on the news that traffic was blocked for over an hour in the direction you normally take. Or, perhaps when you had lunch with a dear friend you sensed something was off, even though he didn't offer any information to confirm the accuracy of your intuitive hit. When he later confides to you that he feared his job was in jeopardy, your sense of "I *knew* something wasn't right!" is validated.

We are all made from the fabric of energy and therefore possess the ability to feel the energetic vibrations moving in and through ourselves, others, and environmental atmospheres. How many times have you said to yourself, "I'm not comfortable with that person's energy," or "Let's get out of this place—I just don't like the vibe in here." Whether or not you were able to pinpoint the "why" of your feelings, "what" you picked up on your inner radar was worthy of your wise attention and action. That "what" emanated from your clairsentience speaking to you, a subject we will cover in depth in the next chapter.

Bringing It All Home

INTROSPECTION

In *Theaetetus*, Plato's dialogue concerning the nature of knowledge, he asks, "Why should we not calmly and patiently review our own thoughts and thoroughly examine and see what these appearances in us really are?" I appreciate his use of the words "really are," which is about going deeper within to become better self-acquainted with what is actually transpiring beneath the appearances in our lives. His is a classic definition of the practice of introspection.

In these postmodern times we might refer to introspection as a practice of self-reflection or self-contemplation, processes we consciously or unconsciously employ when we journal our inner thoughts, feelings, intentions, aspirations, and so on. It is the opposite of "extrospection," which is the observation of what is outside oneself—like people watching, external entertainment, and so on. Introspection causes us to become more conscious and insightful in all aspects of our lives, offering us a deeper awareness as we develop this ability to observe ourselves in a more objective way.

From the application of introspection in my own spiritual practice, I have seen how it surpasses learning from trial and error. Introspection supports us in objectively identifying the intentions and motivations that underlie our actions, allowing us to choose more enlightened interactions with ourselves, others, and our world. As well, we can begin to identify and appreciate more those areas in which we are living up to our self-expectations of honesty, loving kindness, patience, compassion, creativity, generosity of heart, discernment.

I recommend introspecting in the evening after your tasks have been accomplished, because it is quiet and therefore conducive to turning within. Of course, if your daily routine supports introspecting at another time of day, then go with that.

Here are some simple suggestions you may use to set an introspective atmosphere and begin your practice:

+ Select a quiet location where you won't be disturbed for at least twenty or thirty minutes.
+ Gather helpful materials such as your journal, a paper and pen, or a computer to capture what comes up for you.
+ Sit comfortably, relaxed, yet remaining open and alert. You may want to meditate for five or so minutes to center yourself and establish a harmonic balance in body, mind, and spirit, feeling and thought.
+ Begin to write. Do not let the ego judge, censor, or edit your content. Hold back nothing, being as raw and honest as your true feelings are. Simply allow a free flow, a stream of consciousness to express through you. Be sure to be balanced in the sense that in addition to those things that could be improved upon, you also include events wherein you lived your values, where you showed up at the right place at the

right time and said the right things, where you were
of service to others, where you changed a course of
action by listening to guidance.
+ After you feel complete, appreciate and give thanks
for the insights that came through to you and set
your aspirations for the new day ahead.

Related to introspective journaling is the practice of automatic writing. While it takes more practice and is best learned
through a qualified specialist in this field, I offer it here so that
you may determine if you would like to learn more about it
now or at a later time.

AUTOMATIC WRITING

Also referred to as "spirit writing," automatic writing is the
process of producing writing without conscious thought
about what is being written. It is a channeling technique that
invites your spirit guides and/or higher self to step in and write
through you. Either written on a computer or in a journal,
the words are transferred energetically from your sixth sensory
consciousness using your hands to transmit the information.

An art and science in itself, if automatic writing calls to
you, I recommend studying it separately from this book as
what is offered below is, so to speak, the tip of the iceberg. That
being said, even if you have never tried it before, you may still
benefit from the foregoing technique.

+ Whether you are sitting at your computer or at a
table with pen and paper, select a time when you will
not be interrupted by people, your phone, or other

means of intrusion. Turn off the radio, etc., and give your full attention to the process.

+ Open your writing session with a prayerful evocation to your guides and higher self, inviting them to come forth and create an atmosphere of high vibrational energy. Affirm your openness, availability, and surrender to them and the process.

+ With your eyes closed, present one question at a time and patiently await a response. Without editing, interpreting, judging, or censoring what begins to come through, record it on the computer or on paper. Note that even if nothing comes through in the moment, it may pop in when you least expect it, so you may want to carry a pen and paper in your briefcase, pocket, or purse, or have your laptop within close reach.

+ When you feel complete, pause for another five to ten minutes to be sure no further guidance is coming through. In closing, express your gratitude for what has been transmitted to you by spirit, your guides, and higher self.

+ Gently open your eyes and feel yourself reentering your body and the room. Don't jump up to return to the tasks that await you or shock your senses by turning on the television or getting on the phone. Take a few deep breaths before you resume normal activity.

+ When you review your automatic writing, don't be concerned whether or not it makes immediate sense to you. Simply set it aside and read it again later.

✳

CHAPTER 2

Revelations of the
Mystical Mirror

THE PATH TO authentic living is much more profound than most of us have ever been taught. It can be a lifelong process to let go of the cultural myths we have inherited about who we should be, about what our lives should look like. Society has handed us a faulty map for navigating the terrain of our lives, detouring us onto self-constricting paths of guilt, fear, shame, confusion, dogmatism, anxiety, self-doubt, and depression. (And that's the short list!) It's no wonder, then, that what clients most commonly seek from sessions with me is the relief that comes from the reassurance that the totality of their past and present experiences—both positive and negative—are *integral*, vital contributors on their path to self-discovery.

Wise acceptance of this fact allows a letting go of accusations and judgments of ourselves, a healing with loved ones and seeming enemies, as well as a clarifying and resolving of issues with those who have transitioned to the invisible side of life. When this process is activated, the megadoses of self-reproach we mentally feed ourselves soften, labels and stigmas begin to drop away. We realize that we are and always have been worthy of our own love, respect, unconditional compassion, and acceptance.

Once you accept the stunning grace of being guided, which accompanies and caresses you at every turn, you will stand in an unconditional "Yes" to your existence. Your "Whys?" will transmute into "Yesses." With the "I am guided" mantra as your companion, you will travel more willingly into uncharted territories because you recognize that they are tailor-made for awakening your awareness. When a thirsty traveler discovers that her suitcase is filled with lifesaving water, every drop is savored. Likewise, each one of us is a Divine traveler in the human dimension, and when we discover the fathomless depth of the well of our intuitive life, our thirst is quenched from the very root of our being.

The most powerful preparatory gift you can give yourself for entering the sacred portal to your essential self is coming face-to-face with the revelations that are to be found in working with what I call the *mystical mirror*. This work is best described as turning within and intuitively "seeing" in the mirror of your soul the reflection of your true self, of perceiving the purpose for which you have taken a human incarnation, and the specific inner work that is yours to do in this lifetime.

Methods for working with your mystical mirror are described throughout this book. They are specifically designed for quieting the ceaseless mental dialogue, or mind chatter— the repetitious story lines, the inner gossip you create and tell about yourself, others, and the world around you. Why is this so essential? Because it clears from your mind, heart, and spirit lifetimes of dust and debris, allowing you to peer into the mystical mirror of your being with crystal clarity. You become sensitized and attuned to more subtle states of consciousness, elevating your capacity to transmit questions and receive responses from your intuition and spirit guides.

I encourage you to apply loving patience in this process, because it cannot be forced, coerced, or bribed. It is a beautiful, joyful, disciplined practice. And that is why this book includes spiritual practices that will take you beyond the boundaries of your exterior self into the boundless interior of your spirit self.

You see, coming face-to-face with ourselves in deep intimacy through mystical mirroring is the path of a spiritual warrior, one that has been walked by mystics, shamans, Tibetan oracles, mediums, guides, yogis, enlightened beings, and practitioners across all traditions for thousands of years. And here's the best news: As you move closer to becoming more intimate with yourself, you will bravely, gratefully welcome the many revelations, synchronicities, and graces that will emerge.

Yes, there will be times when, with lightning speed, you will want to run away from the revelations in that mirror or shatter it with mental blows and curses. And that is why you will find the practices at the end of each chapter supportive in keeping your seat, regardless of what is reflected in the mirror. It is a process, a slow, gentle, and compassionate process that can be challenging to be patient with in our age of instant gratification at the mere press of a button. When we think of the Buddha's temptations by Mara, of Jesus's forty days and nights in the desert, who are we that we should be given a free ticket to awakened awareness? I don't say this to discourage you, but to *encourage* you by realizing that your every stage of evolutionary progress is sacred.

It cannot be overemphasized that mystical mirroring is neither a test nor a performance. *It is a meditation in which you stand naked before your spirit-soul with the utmost unconditional respect for all that you see, with all that is revealed to you about yourself and your soul's path.*

Harry Potter Got It Right

Can mirrors be used as gateways into other universes and the inner space of Self? Journalist Mark Pendergrast, author of *Mirror Mirror*, had this to say in an interview: "The story of mirrors goes from the Big Bang to the most futuristic use of mirrors in space or nanotechnology. It's possible that invisible 'mirror universes' were created in the moment following the first explosive burst." He goes on to say that in 1610, "the year Galileo saw the moons of Jupiter with his telescope—magic and science finally split, although mirrors remain central to both subjects to this day."[1]

If you're a fan of the Harry Potter series, you may remember that the Mirror of Erised was described by Albus Dumbledore as revealing the "deepest, most desperate desire of our hearts." Did you happen to notice that "Erised" is "desire" spelled backward, the way in which it would be reflected in a mirror? The writing around the Mirror of Erised's frame is equally interesting. When translated it means, "I show not your face but your heart's desire." Harry discovered this when, while wearing his father's invisibility cloak, he came upon the mirror when he ran from a restricted section of the library. Gazing into it, Harry was awestruck by seeing himself surrounded by his deceased parents and other relatives, which, as Dumbledore asserted, was a reflection of the "deepest, most desperate desire of his heart"—conscious or unconscious—to connect with his family on the other side.

As it turns out, Harry is in impressive company. It's recorded that since antiquity mirrors have been used for divination, or *scrying* as it was then called. The Greek philosopher Pythagoras was said to possess a magic mirror which he held up to the moon to see the future. From the Aztecs, Olmecs, Mayans, and Tarascans to medieval wizards and Greek priestesses, mirrors were used as conduits of the supernatural. Mathematician and scientist John Dee, an alchemist and court adviser to Queen Elizabeth I, used a mirror for divination and talking to angels, and was credited with prophesying the plot to kill King James in 1605. He joins the mystics and prophets of old who were convinced that a concave mirror empowers a person's clairvoyant ability.

The power of mirrors also features strongly in feng shui, the ancient Asian art of arranging one's home, which in recent times has become popular with contemporary architects, interior decorators, and homeowners in the West. Mirrors are considered to bring calm into the home environment because they have the same reflective effect as the element of water. Feng shui places mirrors where they will fill a home with beneficial energies and redirect coagulated energy to a more harmonious flow.

It could be said that as far as human inventions go, the mirror is one of the first technologies for self-contemplation and self-revelation, for beyond the vanity of physical self-assessment, a mirror reflects back to us our tapestry of moods, feelings, and energy. Can you recall a time when, standing before a mirror, you penetrated your reflection so intensely you felt certain you could unravel a mysterious aspect of yourself, if only you stood peering into that mirror long enough, deeply enough?

Unpacking Your Birth Suitcase

If you were to ask me, "Hans, in your over fifty years of working with clients and students, what has been the one essential message you most desire to transmit to them?" More poetically than any words can describe, beyond the mind's logic or rationality, from the moment of accepting my calling as a medium, my wholehearted aspiration has been to hold up a mystical mirror in which individuals come face-to-face with their exquisiteness, their imperfect perfection, just as they are.

Just one glimpse into the reality of your true being will cause you to bend a knee before the immaculate conception of cosmic creation that you are. In that glimpse you will not find cherished beliefs or opinions, no spiritually interpretive overlays. Instead, you will come into direct contact with your true self, beyond the illusion of personal identity. Then searching will cease, and a conscious, full-out living of your life will begin. What we are truly seeking is the end of "the search," the end of chasing after the phantoms we are told will guarantee us unending happiness, success, redemption, salvation, even enlightenment. Then, at last, we can finally relax, exhale into a consciousness of utter contentment as we continue our ongoing evolutionary process.

Would it come as a surprise to you that everything you require to actualize this level of profound contentment accompanied you in your birth suitcase, along with the mystical mirror? *Birth suitcase* is a metaphorical term I feel best symbolizes that which we carry with us on each of our incarnational sojourns to the three-dimensional plane. In the suitcase is our soul's individualized blueprint which points to our *dharma*—our unique purpose and the path to its fulfillment, and our *karma*—the accrued effects from lifetimes that draw to us the people, circumstances, etc., that comprise and impact our soul's inner work. The mystical mirror is also included in our birth suitcase of spiritual technologies as the self-reflective faculty of the soul. These terms are defined in more depth in upcoming chapters, so if they are unfamiliar as you read them now, you will soon be very acquainted with them.

Bringing It All Home

THE MYSTICAL MIRROR PRACTICE

It is in the mystical mirror that the contents of one's birth suitcase are revealed, specifically one's overarching inner life-work and what must be unpacked for its fulfillment. This mirror is not outwardly accessible through the physical body's five senses nor by imagination or visualization; it is inwardly accessible through the intuitive third eye of one's spirit-body.

+ Gently close your eyes and take a deep, full inhalation through your nose, and slowly exhale through your mouth. After approximately three breaths, you will become aware of your heart softening, opening, and a centering of your awareness.
+ Return to the natural rhythm of breathing through your nose. With your eyes still closed, gently focus your attention at the point in the middle of your

eyebrows, just slightly above the bridge of your nose, looking into what is referred to as the "third eye." At times you may see a golden center surrounded by pulsating dark blue luminescent rays, while at other times it may be perfectly still. There may also be occasions when you don't see a central orb of light but do see its radiant rays. And even if you see no light or rays at all, you can still feel yourself receiving their radiance.

✦ Without effort, force, or manipulation, simply relax and breathe into the effulgence of this reflective light. Bask your entire being in its luminous energy.

✦ When you feel ready, ask your spirit to mirror back to you your life's work, and to grace you with the courage to unpack from your birth suitcase what is necessary for its fulfillment. Be patient, keeping in mind that even if insights are not immediate, they will come when your consciousness is fertile to receive them.

✦ Allow yourself to rest in the embrace of this precious energy for as long as you desire.

✦ To close your practice, slowly lower your gaze, open your eyes, and return your awareness to the external world. Remain sitting with yourself until you feel fully present in your body and to your outer environment. I suggest you record your insights in a journal.

※

CHAPTER 3

The Anatomy of Spirit Guides

IT IS WELL documented that spirit guides have played a significant role in shaping world history. Their transmissions channeled through various categories of readers including mediums, clairaudients, clairvoyants, and psychics have been recorded since ancient times. In my research, I learned that from Egyptian pharaohs to emperors and queens to modern-era British prime ministers, US presidents—including Abraham Lincoln, Woodrow Wilson, Teddy Roosevelt, Franklin Delano Roosevelt, John F. Kennedy, Lyndon Johnson, Ronald Regan, and Bill Clinton—and popes, vicars, and executives of Fortune 500 companies—all have sought out the services of spirit guides and readers. Professional journals and magazines have featured cultural icons including innovators, inventors, and entertainers who have openly employed the services of readers.

Law enforcement has enlisted psychics to help solve crimes and the federal government has funded programs such as Stargate to investigate individual powers of remote viewing. Dale Graff, a physicist and former director of Project Stargate, was interviewed on the *Larry King Live* 2001 talk show, "Are Psychics for Real?" When asked about his work with Stargate on the power of remote viewing—a form of clairvoyant readership—he is recorded in the transcript as saying, "Instead of shoveling it away and saying there is nothing to it—which is a cop-out—we should say, 'How does it work? What is the key to understanding this?' "[1]

Our Cosmic Cheerleaders

Prior to our current incarnation we moved about freely in the finer dimension of the astral realm in a body of light and communicated telepathically. Upon entering the three-dimensional realm, our spirit is at first shocked to find itself encased in the density of the human form with its limitations of movement and communication. And that's just for starters! The good news is we have been fully equipped for the journey of discovering our spiritual birthright, unpacking our birth suitcase, and victoriously fulfilling our life purpose. And we have enthusiastic cheerleaders in the spirit world who are ready to graciously guide our every step.

My work with clients has clearly demonstrated that although missteps may occur along the way, we never permanently lose sight of why we have embarked on the journey itself. Whenever you so choose, your soul-remembrance of why you have taken a human incarnation can be restored.

Whether or not you consciously remember having forged an agreement with your spirit guides before taking your current earthly incarnation, there is no expiration date on your agreement to connect with them and receive their guidance.

If you have not yet sufficiently cultivated the ability to directly communicate with your spirit guides, a medium can transmit their guidance to you. Mediums can also communicate with other inhabitants in the spirit world who are connected to you and hold answers to questions or other important information relevant to your current incarnation.

Our karmic patterns of lifetimes include our talents, skills, evolutionary spiritual growth, attachments, cherished opinions, beliefs, likes, and dislikes—all of which accompany us in our birth suitcase. By accessing the spirit world, a medium can accurately describe the contours and textures of the patterns of our current lifetime, which has the potential to radically alter the basis of our choice making. A medium is a vehicle through whom you can "phone home" and be reminded that you are a unique, individualized expression of our Creator Source, that it caresses you at every turn, cheers you on, and supports you in every possible way, including through your spirit guides and mediums.

The Integrity Code of Readers and Clients

Some individuals who believe in reincarnation get all caught up in who they might have been in their past lives. Hoping to receive validation that they played a significant role on the world stage, they seek out as many mediums as it takes to meet their desire to hear how they earned name, fame, and fortune. Now exactly how many Cleopatras, William Shakespeares, Mary, Queen of Scots, Mother Teresas, or Rudolph Valentinos have graced the planet? According to some psychics and past-

life regressionists, quite a few! Regrettably, there are unscru-
pulous mediums who tell clients what their egos want to hear.

Whether you are seeking the services of a medium out of
playful curiosity or for profound purposes, it is important to
understand what I call the Law of Equivalents: The motivation
for seeking the services of a medium emits a specific vibrational frequency which draws into one's magnetic field a medium of the same vibrational frequency. Simply put, when you
send out an energetic signal, it attracts its energetic equivalent.

The medium-client relationship is one of co-creation and
co-responsibility. Throughout my fifty plus years of working
with clients, they have entrusted me with the most intimate
details of their lives and the deepest yearnings of their hearts.
Such vulnerability demands the utmost integrity and impeccability on the part of the medium. The client's holistic
well-being is inviolable, requiring confidentiality, nonjudg-
ment about the messages transmitted from the spirit world,
and entrusting the client with full responsibility for the actions
they take based on the guidance provided in the reading. A
bona fide reader recognizes the sanctity of client relationships,
describes the services they offer honestly and clearly, and states
fees for services and products up front. Equally important, the
medium always gives the client back to him or herself by not
permitting an unhealthy dependency to develop.

The responsibilities of clients include educating themselves
on the categories of medium services to ensure which will best
serve them, and then selecting a reputable professional by ob-
taining recommendations from trustworthy sources. I cannot
overemphasize the importance of recommendations. Far too
many times I have witnessed the disillusionment and despair
when desperation leads a person to seek out a medium—*any*

reader—with Holy Grail zeal, only to find an individual of questionable intention and/or skill masquerading as the real deal. Just as you would conduct thorough research in selecting a physician who specializes in a specific field of medicine and obtain references from reliable sources, so is that degree of due diligence required when choosing a reader.

Once having selected a qualified medium, being completely honest in your sharing with him or her is essential to honoring the sacred contract between you, which is one of mutual trust. Testing readers by providing false information is a useless, immature approach, not to mention a waste of your money and their skills. Uncompromised honesty contributes to receiving a pure inflow of guidance.

The inquiries I receive about my services as a medium have brought to my attention that individuals tend to lump together in one category the terms "spirit guide," "medium," "psychic," "clairvoyant," and "clairaudient," primarily because they consider them to be synonymous and their services similar. In a spirit of clarification, I offer the following descriptions as a guide to the services offered and the skills utilized in these primary categories:

+ **Spirit Guides:** Individuals living in the spirit world with whom we shared a relationship while we were inhabiting the fourth dimension and with whom we made an agreement before returning to the Earth plane that they will guide us in a specific aspect or aspects of our present incarnation.
+ **Mediums:** Individuals on the Earth plane with the ability to receive clairaudient messages from the spirit world with the utmost accuracy, completely free of

interference from their human limitations. Mediums
are always psychic but psychics are not always
mediums.

+ **Clairaudients:** Individuals on the Earth plane with
the ability to receive auditory messages from the
spirit world either inwardly by the soul or outwardly
through distinct words or voices. Their level of
accuracy is determined by the level of interference
from their human limitations.

+ **Clairvoyants:** Individuals on the Earth plane with
the intuitive ability to receive messages from the
spirit world by seeing with the eye of the soul images,
words, and/or symbols. Their level of accuracy is
determined by the degree of interference from their
human limitations.

+ **Psychics:** Individuals on the Earth plane with the
clairsentient ability to intuitively communicate with
the spirit world and interpret its messages. Their
accuracy is affected by their human limitations
and their ability to differentiate between genuine
guidance and mind chatter.

+ **Clairsentients:** All human beings possess the
quality of clairsentience, or intuition, by which they
empathetically perceive, feel, and read energy within
themselves, others, and environmental atmospheres.
This innate ability can be consciously accessed,
trained, and deepened.

Bringing It All Home

RETRACING YOUR FOOTSTEPS HOME

An important point in this practice is not to over-try. Just allow yourself to explore the unique terrain of consciousness that is the home of your true Self. You may want to have a journal at hand to record your responses.

- In a location where you won't be disturbed, get into a comfortable position, letting the weight go from your body while remaining alert.
- Take a long inhalation through your nose and slowly exhale through your mouth, repeating this three to four times or until your body begins to relax.
- Visualize yourself as you were around the age of four, as this will support you in connecting to a pristine state of being prior to the influence of societal conditioning. (It may help to have on hand a photograph of yourself close to that age.)
- Feel into your "home," your core self, and invite it to inform you about the dharma and karma that accompanied you in your birth suitcase. Examples might include: What did I come on the planet to learn and do? Am I aligned with that purpose? What is the next step in my evolutionary progress? (You may also want to revisit the mirroring exercise at the end of chapter 2.)
- When you are ready, gently open your eyes and return to the outer world. Take all the time you need to assimilate your experience. Journal any insights

you received and were guided to act upon. Note that
it is not unusual for guidance to come through your
intuition days or even weeks after this exercise.

✦ Appreciate yourself for your courage to retrace your
footsteps home and the willingness to follow through
on what is revealed to you.

To enhance and expand your learning of intuitive development, visit the link below for free resources:
www.GuidedBook.com/guides

CHAPTER 4

✳

Fine-Tuning Your Clairsentience

PREPARE TO HEAR this theme reverberating throughout the pages of this book: *Clairsentience is our spiritual inheritance.* Even in our postmodern world, where technological gizmos direct our driving, identify the nearest Thai restaurant, reserve our theater tickets, pay our bills, all of this outer practicality is subservient to the inner practicality of our intuitive voice, our clairsentience. Our Divine Source has accessorized all beings with clairsentience; it is encrypted in our consciousness awaiting our recognition and activation. This means, dear reader, that even if you are a naysayer, doubter, or somewhere in the middle, you are not an exception to possessing clairsentience. It may lay dormant within you, but be assured it is there.

Clairsentience is not something you have to ask for, hope for, or wait for. It is not the result of the DNA of a psychic family member, random event, or a transformative, energetic shift that will happen one day through your spiritual practice. In other words, clairsentience is not a future goal; it is a present-moment reality awaiting your consent to be activated within you, just as you are in the here and now. When it comes to trusting your faculty of clairsentience, being economical turns out to be an expensive choice, and denying its existence is a waste of a highly valuable resource.

When first activating your clairsentience it requires practice, just as does the development of any other skill, and you can count on there being hits and misses. It can be compared to learning how to fine-tune a shortwave radio. In the beginning the communication squeaks and squawks, goes in and out; however, if you are persistent, with just a very light touch you will eventually receive clear communication. As you develop and refine your clairsentience, you also accelerate the vibrational frequency through which you receive guidance from your spirit guides, which you will learn in more detail in the next chapter.

You have been calibrated to receive direct communication transmitted from your spirit guides through your clairsentience. Listening to and following its guidance isn't for the weak at heart; it is for those who are courageous and spiritually mature enough to look at the whole picture of their lives and apply what is shared from the other side.

As you feel into the material in this chapter, can you perceive how your life would shift if you were willing to devote the time and disciplined practice required to work with your guides? It bears repeating that the ability to receive guidance from spirit and your guides is most effective when you first unclutter your own consciousness so that you may learn how to listen and hear differently. And believe me when I say your guides are just as eager to begin their work with you as you are with them. As already mentioned, they have been assigned to you and they want to succeed at their assignment so that they, too, may progress in their evolutionary process!

Clairsentience and Your Guides

Some of you who are reading this page may already have begun to discover and activate your birthright of clairsentient, clairvoyant, and/or clairaudient abilities. Or perhaps you may be making that discovery as you read and practice the principles in this book. Whatever the case, as you cleanse and thereby clarify your consciousness through your inner work, it will profoundly enhance your capacity to consciously work with spirit and your guides. That is why I reiterate—perhaps to the point of annoyance, and if so, kindly bear with me—how important it is to devote your energies to your spiritual practices. Your guides cannot do the work for you, and no authentic reader will shortchange you by claiming there's no work for you to do except just believe their reading. A medium of impeccability will always, without exception, give you back to yourself, will self-empower you.

I encourage you to work with your spirit guides in identifying, refining, and expanding your intuitive capacity, because as your sixth sense of clairsentience becomes more precise, your access to the invisible side of life will amplify. This is not an imaginational experience. Just behind the denser vibratory field of the third dimension is the finespun, subtle realm of the fourth dimension. I encourage you, dear one, to look not outwardly or upwardly at the sky, but rather to turn within and soul-quest the spirit world as a means of realizing that even as our feet are firmly planted on Earth, we remain simultaneously connected to the heavenly realm.

Isn't it comforting to know that you may call upon your spirit guides 24/7 and never be greeted by a recorded message, transferred to voice mail, get stuck on hold, or be disconnected? Spirit energy is constant—it doesn't have an off switch! But what does cause interference in our communication with the invisible realm is the static emanating from our end of the conversation. That "static" is mind chatter, the great interloper. Your soul has deeper things to say to you and about you, but they cannot be heard by remaining on the surface of mind chatter.

Mind Chatter: The Great Saboteur

Mind chatter was not packed in your birth suitcase. It was pumped in from the outside of you by societal conditioning and it's high time to learn how to skillfully tame it. Reflect on this for a moment: Why do we have the television on when we're not even watching it; why do we play music and not really listen to it; why do we seek constant entertainment under the guise of "relaxing"? We live in the Age of Distraction, using whatever it takes to drown out the anguish of hurts, disappointments, betrayals, insecurities, of a life not fully lived.

The need to be constantly entertained was implanted within us long before today's social media came along, and is accepted as being perfectly normal and natural. So normal, in fact, that we participate mindlessly, without questioning why quiet makes us squirm, get edgy, jump up and find something, *anything*, to do that allows us to drown out the inner voice that says "I hurt." We perpetually seek to avoid the sharp thorns of underlying anxiety, fears, the unattended pain in our hearts, and instead fill our life with the noise of distraction and mind chatter.

We have been programmed to believe that spending time in our own company is undesirable, that it is something to avoid rather than a healthy way of getting to know ourselves and learning how to enjoy our own company. "An idle mind is the devil's workshop," we are taught. Why? Because we might begin to think as an independent individual rather than blindly following the collective beliefs of society, politicians, and religious dogmas that insist people must be controlled to create an orderly, well-functioning society.

Societal conditioning from family, education, religion, government, movies, television, peers, and social media is intended to establish itself as the supreme authority about what is right and good for us. It is filled with lies about: Who we should be. How we should look. What we should wear. How we should smell. What pharmaceuticals will restore our health, virility, and sexiness even when their side effects potentially include death. What profession will give us prestige and power. What we should drive. Where we should live. What's hot and what's not. Anything different from those choices and achievements is a reflection of our personal failure and irrelevance to society. It's enough to make you run away to a Himalayan cave!

We live far, far away from the Buddhist adage "Don't just do something—sit there!" Yes, sit there, and with attentive compassion and loving kindness practice being honest with yourself about all the mind chatter you run and act upon. Then, without judgment, commit to learning how to identify it, skillfully work with it, and with genuine humor to laugh at it. I share these words to metaphorically shake and wake you so that you can begin to catch when societal conditioning—and its henchman mind chatter—detour you from your authentic path. And the encouraging news is that once you learn to work skillfully with them, you can get right back on track to fulfilling the life purpose encrypted in your karma and dharma.

Taming the Chatterbox Syndrome

My years of countless readings for clients have provided a flood of evidence that the mind chatter syndrome deserves in-depth attention, so in this chapter and throughout this book you will find various time-tested methods that will support you in achieving freedom from this tyrant.

I was amused to learn that the term "chatterbox" dates back to 1774 and was originally considered to be "a container full of idle talk." In today's popular usage it describes an overtalkative person. But the mind's chatterbox syndrome is not limited to outer verbosity; it is equally applicable to our mental monologues with and about ourselves, others, and life in general.

Mind chatter—that static buzz in the background and sometimes the foreground of our mind—is exhausting, energy depleting, and undermining. Because mind chatter also lodges itself in our subconscious mind, even in sleep and in the dream state we aren't spared its harassment. The most challenging aspect is the automatic assumption that the lies spewing out of the mind's chatterbox are true! A tricky contributor to this belief is that we inwardly hear chatter in the sound of our own voice, which we totally identify with.

How easy it is to be swept away by the toxic sea of mind

chatter flowing in our minds. In addition to the life jacket of our spiritual practices, cultivating a sense of humor is highly effective. Here is a simple yet skillful method: With great passion, holding nothing back, repeat your mind chatter out loud until you *really hear and feel* the ridiculousness of the things you tell yourself about yourself, others, and the circumstances in your life.

Your chatter is not your conscience advising you. It is not your guides or spirit conversing with you. It is a dysfunctional energy vampire that has no power or credibility except that which you give it. Use your sense of humor to disempower mind chatter and reempower yourself.

Perceiving Your Perceptions

One definition of the word "perception" comes from the Latin word *percipere*, meaning "to seize." And that's precisely what occurs as you perceive your perceptions: You seize your mind chatter, metabolize it into your perceptions, and your mind convinces you it is true. But mere perceptions are vastly different from the purity of the direct revelations that come to us from the sixth sense of clairsentience, be it our own or in communication with our spirit guides or a medium.

Throughout my years as a medium, after working with over fifty thousand individuals from all walks of life, I've observed that no one is free from running their mind chatter. A high-powered businessman who attended one of my seminars later confided to me: "When you were describing how to tame mind chatter, I knew it would work. But the truth is, I thought you were talking to everyone else in the room except

me, because I considered myself above it. Then, in the very
next second, I realized that arrogant thought came directly
from my mind chatter and I had a good, humbling laugh at
myself." How poignantly he reveals that the starting point for
quieting your chatter is right on the spot where you now stand.

There are also valuable insights about your neurotic ten-
dencies being revealed in your mental chatter: what triggers
and hooks you, what you obsess about, where you get stuck
in fear and other limiting thoughts about your appearance,
religion, sexuality, relationships, credentials or lack thereof,
your dreams, successes, failures, your life's résumé—labels you
trust as being accurate.

I encourage you to take a moment and ask yourself: "Do
the labels I place on aspects of my life resonate with who I
am today? Is it time to press the pause button on the mind
chatter that runs me ragged and discern if any of it is actually
the truth?"

Mind chatter can be likened to weeds in a garden. You may
spend a lot of time nurturing your plants and flowers, but if you
don't tend to the weeds they will eventually overtake the garden.

By the time we reach chronological adulthood, we have
fertilized our mind chatter to such a degree that we've grown
comfortable with how its weeds have overtaken us. So comfortable, in fact, that if it quiets down we feel like something
is missing. We begin looking for our mind chatter as though
for a lost beloved friend. When day after day we brutally repeat our self-critical mind chatter of the could've, should've,
would've blaming and shaming, we don't realize how we are
terrorizing ourselves—and perhaps others as well—with this
great saboteur.

If it is your sincere intention to bloom a beautiful mental, emotional, and spiritual Garden of Eden within your spirit, then you will have to pick the weeds of mind chatter. And there's no moment like the present to begin!

Bringing It All Home

The following practices are for the purpose of establishing a solid foundation for attuning to higher states of consciousness by accelerating the development of your clairsentience and actualizing the practical joys of communicating with your guides. Combined with the Mystical Mirror practice described in chapter 2, they constitute the secret sauce that has been time tested by spiritual savants and practitioners across all spiritual traditions for fulfilling one's karma and dharma, for living in the unbroken realm of conscious connection to Pure Spirit, even as one's feet are firmly planted on earthly ground.

MORNING ALIGNMENT EXERCISE

When you first wake up, you are still sensitized to the vibration of the finer astral realm, making it an auspicious time to pause and, even for as short a time as five minutes, consciously enter the new day grounded in your spirit-soul. The morning is our opportunity to set the energetic pattern of our day, and the more present we are as we enter it, in that alertness, our aligned connection to the other side will carry, guide, guard, and caress us with its grace.

+ Lying on your back in your bed, place your arms
  along each side of your body. With your eyes closed

or open, take a long inhalation through your nose
while gently tensing your entire body; hold it for
three seconds. Exhale through your mouth while
simultaneously releasing the tension. Next, feel the
warmth of the life force circulating in your body
temple. Repeat this exercise three times.

✦ Out loud or silently, call your own name, as though
it were a sacred mantra: "Maria, are you here?" Then
answer, "Yes, I am here," and feel the entirety of your
being fully present in your response.

✦ Next, in the language of your own heart, express your
gratitude to spirit and your guides for being with you
throughout the night and escorting you into the new
day.

✦ Close the exercise by affirming along these lines: In
this moment and throughout the day, I attune myself
to the voice in my soul, to spirit and guidance. This
nourishment comes from the openness of my own
heart.

✦ Throughout various times of the day, remember to
pause and again call your own name, which will cause
a gap in your mind chatter, bringing your awareness
into the present moment.

MEDITATION

Meditation is not a doing but rather a state of being, of residing in one's core self. Meditation offers us the opportunity to
realize that the higher self of our self is the witness, the observer of what is observed. As we touch this core self, we catch
that our spirit-soul is the host, and that our human self, with

its personality traits, mindsets, habits, attachments, cherished beliefs, enjoyments, etc., is the guest.

Meditation complements any spiritual tradition you may be affiliated with and opens your heart to the Divine's presence. I recommend avoiding those ads inviting you to "Learn how to meditate like a Buddhist monk in just twenty minutes." (I can't help but wonder why, then, monks and nuns devote an entire lifetime to deepening their practice!) If you don't already have a meditation practice, ask spirit for guidance as to what would best suit you at this stage in your journey. What follows is a Buddhist shamatha technique. *Shamatha* means a tranquil, calm-abiding, stabilizing meditation.

+ Begin by taking a meditation posture either on a floor cushion or a chair. If you are sitting on a floor cushion, make sure your hips are elevated enough so that your back is not slumping and your knees rest flat on the cushion. If your preference is a chair, make sure it has a straight back. Sit forward in the chair so your feet are flat on the floor. Whether you're on a cushion or chair, keep your spine erect but without straining or overarching your back. Place your hands on your thighs with your palms facing up or down.

+ If you wish, close your eyes. If not, lower your gaze and place it just about four feet in front of you. If closing your eyes causes you to feel sleepy, then it's best to practice with a lowered, open-eyed gaze. If sleepiness intrudes, reset your gaze a few feet more in front of you, or look straight ahead for a few seconds and then lower your gaze once again.

+ Now place your attention on the breath. Begin
  by slowly taking two or three deep inhalations/
  exhalations, remaining aware of the air as it enters
  and exits your nostrils. Then continue breathing
  in your natural rhythm. Be with the breath as it
  happens, one breath at a time.
+ Mind chatter in the form of thoughts, emotions,
  and fantasies will arise, which is perfectly natural.
  Sometimes you will spin out for a while before
  realizing that your attention is no longer on the
  breath. Without judgment, mentally say "thinking,"
  and with loving patience bring your awareness back
  to the breath.
+ Do something to signify the end of your sitting,
  whether it be reading an inspiring quote, a closing
  chant, a respectful bow before a home altar if you
  have one, ringing a gong, or a prayer of gratitude
  to your guides, teachers, and the teachings you are
  practicing.

A brief word about the aftereffects of meditation is in order.
Through practice, as you contact and expand that "soft spot"
within you, you may find yourself becoming more sensitive
to other individuals, animals, nature, and television news as it
broadcasts the tremendous suffering of our brothers and sisters
in different parts of the world. Likewise, your sensitivity to
the humanitarian good done in the world where people, animals, and nature are concerned also becomes more sensitized.
When you feel this wave of open-heartedness, welcome it, put
it to compassionate use by sending healing energy, healing
thoughts wherever they are needed, and gratitude for those

who are performing compassionate humanitarian service in the world.

PRAYER

Prayer arises from our trust in a power and presence that is ever available, utterly approachable, compassionate, ready to respond to our prayers through the laws governing the universe, laws based on unconditional love.

When we pray affirmatively, we omit the vocabulary of doubt, beggary, or demands that spirit be our custom-made delivery service, catering to our every whim. That being said, we all have those biblical "Job-like" moments that literally or metaphorically bring us to our knees, when only an anguished prayer tantrum arises from within us and we give spirit a piece of our minds! The truth is, there is no right or wrong way to pray other than to be authentic, knowing that whether it's anger, grief, joy, gratitude—any emotion, spirit can handle it, because it knows our hearts.

Prayer is not always about asking for something, for making a specific request. There are times when a spontaneous desire arises in the heart simply to express our love to the Divine Beloved of our soul, to surrender into its intoxicating embrace. When the Presence is so tangible we feel it will take form right before our eyes—as it has for mystics across spiritual traditions—that is the time to drop whatever we are doing and be fully present to that precious moment of such stunning grace.

In general, I offer no prayer "rules," for ultimately prayer is expressed in the language of the heart, spoken from the intimacy of one's uniquely personal relationship with spirit.

Eventually, that time comes when the prayer prays you. Then prayer ceases and holy communion begins.

Now, when our prayer requests are specifically directed to our guides, it is important to keep in mind that they have what I call the "blueprint" of our dharma and karma and respond accordingly. This means that we may receive a different response to our prayer than anticipated, but be assured it will reflect what represents our ultimate good.

SPIRITUAL STUDY

Spiritual study goes hand-in-hand with your spiritual practice as far as deepening your spiritual development. Spiritual study goes far beyond being entertained by reading a spiritually themed book during leisure time. Genuine study can even be a bit annoying to the ego because it offers consciousness-stretching challenges.

From the perspective of reading for the purpose of spiritual growth, it is wise to understand that as the reader you are making an energetic connection to the author and his or her caliber of consciousness. Applying discernment in the selection of your study materials is not about judgment, for to be discerning is to intuitively grasp whether the teachings, principles, and practices in the book you are considering to study or have begun to study will expand your current level of consciousness.

In addition to your own assessment of your study material, you may request input from your guides through intuition, prayer, or a medium. It may be that they will direct you to books, videos, or CDs by teachers you never would have sought to explore but from which you may greatly benefit.

Here are some tips I've created as a result of countless years of spiritual study:

- ✦ Read the introduction of the book so that you understand the author's intention for writing it, the lineage of spiritual teachers with whom he/she has studied that will also have a vibratory impact on you, and what you may expect to learn from the book's contents.
- ✦ Pause at appropriate sections of the book and ask yourself whether you are grasping the significance of its main points.
- ✦ When you feel that a poignant section of the text is clear to you, confirm it by explaining it to yourself in your own words.
- ✦ Highlight sections that especially speak to you. Test them in the laboratory of your own life by putting them into practice. Go back and reread them from time to time, because that is an excellent way to observe your progress, since our capacities increase with practice.

CHAPTER 5

✳

Spirit Guides:
Ambassadors of Awakening

COMMUNICATING WITH those in the spirit world isn't about getting into an altered state or speaking in high-consciousness language for the sake of making a favorable impression or earning favors. Our communication with the other side is about authenticity, a coming from the heart without filtering or bypassing what needs to be expressed through us in a down-to-earth, vulnerable, raw, and honest manner.

You can even use four-letter words when raging against heart-wrenching loss and grief, reconciling old conflicts, and making amends with departed loved ones over past hurts. It may not always be a soothing hot tub experience, and yet it is encouraging to know that when we cross over, we receive clarifying insights into our un-Buddha-like moments, making it possible to continue doing forgiveness and healing work from both sides of the veil.

Now I simply can't resist including a few more examples that don't constitute a breach of etiquette when communicating with spirit guides. You needn't wear crystals or prayer beads, dab on purifying oils or powders, burn incense, sit in full or half lotus, get down on your knees, or bow. Incantations, potions, amulets, pendulums—none of these accoutrements or other gadgetry are required to download intuitive guidance. There are individuals, however, who have come to a session convinced that they must be accessorized with items which they believe are guaranteed to sharpen their intuitive antenna, and mine as well. Admittedly, there have been times when this has caused a spontaneous, good-natured chuckle on my part, along with a compassionate recognition that, as in the examples which follow, for some individuals these accessories create a sense of safety or security, especially if superstition or paranoia have played a part in their lives.

On one occasion a client arrived carrying a loudly buzzing machine, which she claimed would help me to tap into the spirit world with greater potency. One gentleman brought his Chihuahua, because he believed little Snookie would be a channel through which his parents would deliver a message. (I had to explain that although dogs have an innate capacity to pick up energy, due to the high vibrational frequency present during a session, it might be more potent energy than his dog could comfortably metabolize.)

I also had a client who took nearly six months to book his first appointment because he was convinced it had to be made according to the timing prescribed by his tuning fork. When we finally met, he brought the tuning fork with him. At the opening of our sessions, he pressed it against his forehead three times and finally announced, "OK, the fork has indicated we can now proceed."

Then there was a lovely woman in her fifties who arrived wearing a crystal tiara on her head with an amethyst that hung

from it and rested on her third eye, which she explained was
for the purpose of warding off any negative spirits around me.
A man once came accompanied by a garden snake in a mason
jar. "I will know that you are the real thing," he said, "if you
repeat the password to the spirit world that the snake gave to
me as a sure sign that your reading will be authentic."

The main point is that communicating with those on the
other side doesn't produce more powerful results by means of
rituals, scents, or a dress code; it is activated by a soul agreement that was long ago etched across the hearts of its participants, one that is quite ordinary. And by "ordinary" I mean it
can happen *unconditionally*, under any circumstances, even the
most unlikely. When that incomparable reverberation occurs
in your solar plexus, the *manipura* chakra, or the heart, the
anahata chakra, it can occur whether you are sitting on your
meditation cushion, standing at the kitchen sink, feeding your
dog, or mowing the back forty, transporting you into a state of
full trust in what comes next.

Now, I don't at all mean to strip spirit communication of
its sweetness, for just as for very special occasions we prepare
by dressing ourselves in elegant clothing, splashing on lovely
scents, jewelry, and such, so may we prep the mind and body
for entering a sacred ritual as a way of creating an inner ambi-
ence of open-minded and open-hearted receptivity. Creating
a conducive atmosphere for inviting and welcoming one's
guides by, for example, decorating an altar with flowers and
candles is a lovely gesture. And while spirit communication
seems extraordinary, it is ordinary in the sense that it is a
natural human endowment. As Edgar Mitchell, Apollo 14
astronaut and co-founder of the Institute of Noetic Science,
reminds us, "There are no unnatural or supernatural phenom-

ena, only very large gaps in our knowledge of what is natural."

My main point is this: Loyalty to our relationships in the spirit world begins with not turning our backs on or discounting our own clairsentient abilities by placing the power outside of ourselves in accoutrements, gadgets, or rituals.

The Descent of Spirit into Matter

To best grasp the essence of the spirit world and the beings known collectively as spirit guides, it is helpful to first understand what comprises our own essence. Perhaps no one put it better than the French Jesuit philosopher and paleontologist Pierre Teilhard de Chardin, to whom this most apropos quote is attributed: "We are not human beings having a spiritual experience. We are spiritual beings having a human experience." Before the creation of the cosmic spheres and the beings who inhabit them, they existed as vibrational waves of thought-energy emanating from Source. This energy, vibrating at varying frequencies, condensed into form, including yours and mine.

"We are a way for the cosmos to know itself," said Carl Sagan in the first episode of his 1980 PBS documentary *Cosmos*.[1] I dare to interpret him as meaning that through the human being, spirit gets to know what it is like to reach the pinnacle of cosmic consciousness and merge into oneness with itself. In less abstract and more devotional terms, the evolution of our consciousness is a cosmic courtship between our individual soul and spirit. Our spirit guides are the matchmakers whose guidance supports us in removing whatever obstacles block our inner awakening to this Eternal Love Affair. We catch glimpses of this in the intoxicating words of the Divine's mystical lovers such as Rumi when he wrote in his poem "The Meaning of Love":

> *Although I may try to describe Love*
> *when I experience it I am speechless.*[2]

Roll Call and Résumés

How touching it is to know that spirit never forces itself upon us, that through free will it is we who determine that heart-opening moment of surrendering the protective ego to our custom-made guidance system. How momentous is that moment!

That being said, it is now my privilege to introduce you to your spirit guides—please insert a drumroll here—beginning at the top of the hierarchy:

+ **Doorkeeper Spirit Guide:** Your Doorkeeper, an extension of the arm of spirit, has contributed to your spiritual evolutionary progress throughout your incarnations in both the astral and terrestrial realms and will continue to do so until you are a fully liberated being. This supremely evolved spirit ceased reincarnating in the physical realm countless aeons ago and occupies one of the highest levels in the astral realm with occasional vacations in the higher causal realm. Your Doorkeeper directs into your life those guides, teachers, and paths that offer the spiritual practices and life lessons for best fulfilling your karma and dharma, and is the adviser to your Master Guide. As the title indicates, Doorkeepers prevent the entry of spirits that are not assigned to you and entities that are otherwise not meant to be participants in the current stage of your journey.

The depth of your intuitive ability and application of free will contour the twists and turns taken on your path to awakening. Your Doorkeeper does not judge your choices and there are no repercussions with the exception that you will repeat the same life lessons until you learn them. While your Doorkeeper sparks insights, at the end of the day, only you can work with your mind chatter, habits, attachments, and societal conditioning. Now here is some very encouraging news: From your Doorkeeper you receive a compassionate, assisting grace that extends some karmic leeway all along your path.

✦ **Master Spirit Guide:** Your Master Guide holds the blueprint of your karma and dharma, your soul contract of past lifetimes and current incarnation. Its range of impact upon your existence is tremendous, enhanced by consultations with your Doorkeeper. Although Master Guides have evolved beyond the need to incarnate in the three-dimensional realm, they may, out of their own free choice, return to the third dimension for the upliftment of the planet in the role of an avatar or supremely evolved being. But whether in the higher astral realm or on Earth, their assignment is to guide and support those assigned to them in fulfilling their dharma and karma.

A pivotal contribution made by your Master Guide involves your spiritual aspirations and intentions. When you choose to consciously attune yourself to following your dharma, your Master Guide will joyfully step in and, operating through your intuition, guide you to every means of support for fulfilling your aspiration. I have no doubt that by the time you are reading this page you have many times over discovered a book, path, teacher, movie, or a new acquaintance that felt like a purely magical, synchronistic event showing up in your life.

As with your Doorkeeper, your Master Guide never force-feeds you nor gives up on you. Guidance continues to be whispered into your heart-soul with loving kindness, compassion, infinite patience, and just the perfect amount of humor.

+ **Helper Spirit Guides:** Your Helper Spirit Guides operate under your Master Guide. Their assignment is to work with you on transforming the mental and emotional habit patterns that govern your life. *You are your own favorite habit*, and shaking up your habit-driven life is the point at which becoming conscious begins. So Helper Guides use the nitty-gritty details of your everyday existence as vehicles for creating self-awareness. Their guidance is a call to accountability, integrity, self-honesty, and self-empowerment.

Helper Guides live in a mid-level astral realm and do reincarnate in the lower astral realms as required to complete their astral karma. If their astral karma is such that reincarnating in the earthly realm would accelerate their development, their own guides will support them during their karmic commute. But it is when occupying the astral realm that your Master Guide assigns those who qualify to be your Helper Guides. Some are likely to be spirits with whom you have interacted during terrestrial lifetimes or while you were together in the astral realm.

+ **Family and Friend Spirit Guides:** Family members and friends of recent incarnations who transitioned into their next dimension of living did not end their relationship with you upon their departure; these relationships continue to evolve and are even now with you in a companionable, guiding way. During those times when you occupied the astral realm together, you mutually agreed to support one another in specific aspects of your respective earthly sojourns. Your heart is a receiving station wherein you can feel their presence and through which you may communicate with them.

Now, I preface what I am about to say by acknowledging that it may not earn me a lot of "likes" on Facebook, but here goes: Even troublesome, challenging relationships with family and friends doesn't prevent them from being on your team of spirit guides. As earlier mentioned, when we're on the other side we do get insights

into our less-than-noble behaviors of the past and
seek to resolve them, to make amends with family
and friends on the Earth plane. This means that
individuals who fit this description from your current
or relatively recent past lifetimes, and who are now
in the fourth dimension, may tap at the door of your
intuitive awareness, or be guided to you by your
Master or Helper Guide.

Medium-Transmitted Communication from Your Guides

Your entire tribe of guides not only communicates with you
directly, its members also convey messages to you through a
medium. I recommend having a session with a medium from
time to time, particularly in situations when your mind chatter prevents you from connecting with your guides or when
you want validation that you have accurately interpreted what
has come through them from the other side. However, I must
stress that it is not healthy to develop a dependency on a medium any more than it is to become solely dependent upon
a therapist, guru, or any other outer sources for the irreplace-
able, soul-stretching inner work that only you can do.

I would like to now share with you, from the ringside seat
of fifty-five years of experience, how your work with a medium
would unfold in a private session, allowing, of course, for the
unexpected things that not surprisingly enter every session due
to spirit's spontaneity!

I am what is referred to as a direct-voice medium, which
means that as messages from the other side are being trans-

mitted to me, I simultaneously verbalize them—word for word—to my client.

Before a client's arrival—or prior to a session by phone—I center my consciousness and for some time commune with spirit and my guides. Then, during the session, my guides introduce me to the client's guides who convey the messages they wish to communicate along with answers to the client's specific questions. For the most part, it is my master or helper guides who conduct the introductions, which may include the client's master or helper guide, and family and friend spirit guides.

Once the session concludes, the client leaves with clarity and equipped with practical guidance on how to put into practice what was revealed in the session.

In his *Autobiography of a Yogi*, Paramahansa Yogananda writes about a visitation from his deceased guru, Sri Yukteswar, who visited him from the highest astral plane of Hiranyaloka three months after his passing. Here is a brief extract from his description of the astral world: "The ordinary astral universe—not the subtler astral heaven of Hiranyaloka—is peopled with millions of astral beings who have come, more or less recently, from the earth, and also with myriads of fairies, mermaids, fishes, animals, goblins, gnomes, demigods, and spirits, all residing on different astral planes in accordance with karmic qualifications."[3]

So now you know that if a medium tells you that one of your guides has come forward with a parrot on his/her shoulder, a purring Siamese cat, or tail-wagging dog, it's certain to be one of your beloved animal companions who wishes to connect with you and perhaps even deliver a message. In my own experience, rare are the occasions when this doesn't cause an immediate eruption of joyful tears from a client!

Another common question I've been asked by clients concerns contacting loved ones who have reincarnated on Earth soon after their passing. I assure you that when it is to the karmic advantage of you both, they can be located and I describe the process for reconnecting with them in chapter 8.

Bringing It All Home

A TREASURY OF TIPS

A thriving relationship with our spirit guides is one that contains many of the same qualities that form the foundation of any healthy relationship. Respect, love, honesty, trust, attentiveness, acceptance, appreciation, openness, intimacy, patience, generosity, freedom, flexibility, skillfully working through conflict—all of these mindsets and heartsets contribute to the staying power of a committed relationship. You will recognize many of these same qualities included in the following tips for communicating with your spirit guides. Please note that these tips are not in any order of importance—each is an equally significant contributor to building and maintaining a dynamic relationship with your guides.

+ Respecting the sacredness of communicating with your guides means holding your experiences with them close to your heart and not frivolously sharing or bragging about them, just as you would in any intimate human relationship.
+ First thing in the morning, before you get out of bed, send your guides a wink as a gesture of acknowledgment of their presence. It's even better if

you can develop a habit of practicing the Morning Alignment exercise described in chapter 4, even if just for five or ten minutes.

+ Do not strain in your efforts to contact your guides nor attempt to force a response. A relaxed, open state of consciousness works best on both sides of the veil.

+ On occasions when you want to have a formal session with your guides, practice a centering technique such as the meditation described in chapter 4. If you have a light question about one of your daily activities or interactions, you need not sit for a formal session; simply ask the question and go about your day.

+ Whether you've completed a formal session or informal conversation, be sure to express to your guides your gratitude for their unfailing presence and support.

+ Since you are their assignment, your spirit guides want to know they are succeeding or where improvements may be in order. Be open and generous with your feedback.

+ If a particular expression of guidance feels uncomfortable to you, it's not only OK to say so, it's essential.

+ There will be times when you are better able to quiet mind chatter and connect than at others. When mental static overpowers your efforts to communicate, that's when you know it's time to pause and press the refresh button by stilling your mind through the meditation practice described in chapter 4.

+ Ask your guides for their names. If after a few inquiries you receive no response from one or more of them, go ahead and assign a name that you feel is a match for your sense of their presence. Use it consistently and they will respond. Most do announce their title, meaning their role in your life, but if you still have any questions, simply ask.
+ Pass on the temptation to ask for "signs."
+ Spirit has no memory problems, so you needn't broadcast reminders about earlier requests. Nor is spirit hard of hearing. Fourth-dimension clocks tick to Divine right timing, giving us an opportunity to practice trust and patience.
+ Your departed loved ones in the spirit world never tire of hearing from you. It's thoughtful to begin your day by sending them a wink, a smile, and to remember them on the occasion of special anniversaries you celebrated together.
+ Give your friend and helper guides specific assignments. After all, you will probably be touching upon the agreements you already made when you were with them in the spirit world.
+ The highest vibrational request, question, or discussion you can have with your guides is about how you are progressing with the fulfillment of your karma and dharma, and how you may accelerate your inner evolutionary process.
+ Remember that living a spirit-guided life is about partnering with the spirit world and applying this immeasurably valuable resource in your daily life.

CHAPTER 6

✳

Karma and Dharma: Two Sides of the Cosmic Coin

WHEN THE INEVITABLE knock arrives and you are face-to-face with the primal questions "Who am I?" and "Why am I here?," it can feel like an inconvenient speed bump, causing you to slow down and begin your inner quest. Sometimes the knock of awakening arrives in the form of a personal tragedy such as the loss of a loved one, one's health, home, or livelihood. Then again, it may occur as though you're on a smooth, comforting wave during a session with a therapist, rabbi, Tibetan lama, a medium, or during a massage. But of this we can be sure: There is an ineffable Presence traveling within us that will never stop knocking until we open the door, welcome it, and serve the tea of surrender sweetened with the commitment to live our purpose.

According to Dr. Andrew Newberg's pioneering scientific research in the field of neurotheology—the study of the brain and spirituality—the impulse to spiritually question is deeply rooted in the biology of the brain. His initial research included the use of nuclear medical brain imaging to study Buddhist meditators and Franciscan nuns, among others, in prayer. Imagine if such a technology had been around during the time of the Buddha, Lao-Tzu, Krishna, or Jesus—how could anyone resist being curious about what would have been revealed on its monitor?

Why Following Your
Dharma = Good Karma

Dharma is a Sanskrit word for the ultimate law governing the universe through which all existence—from galaxies to human beings—evolves its purpose for being. It is also translated as an individual's place in the cosmic process: in time, in space, in awareness, in thought, and in purpose. *Dharma* also refers to the path that leads us to the fulfillment of our purpose: the conscious realization of our inherently enlightened nature.

You, like every other person walking the planet, have an individual dharmic pathway that is aligned with the karmic patterns that accompanied you in your birth suitcase in this lifetime. However, we are not designed to be forever bound to the three-dimensional world. When we commit to following our dharma, we reap good karma and begin to liberate ourselves from the *samsaric* wheel of birth, death, and rebirth. We graduate! A clear understanding of the complementary relationship between dharma and karma—how they are two sides of the cosmic coin—gives us confidence to continue in the direction our journey is taking us.

Dharma:
The Purpose within Your Purpose

If in this moment you were to ask yourself "What is my purpose?," would you respond from your intellect or your intuition? Your answer is significant, because it reveals your understanding of and your relationship to your life purpose. Those who respond from the intellect most commonly describe their life purpose in terms of a profession: "Even though I teach anthropology, I have such a passion for music I've always known my purpose was to be a musician, but I was afraid I would end up a starving artist." When responding from intuition, there is a more conscious awareness of one's dharmic path: "Even though I have a degree in anthropology, I became a musician not only because of my passion for music, but because I also sensed I'd come in contact with my soul-tribe and experience inner growth." This response comes from an intuitive perception of the *purpose within one's purpose*; it is the fulfillment of the karmic propensity to be a musician while simultaneously fulfilling one's dharma toward becoming an awakened being.

The Mystery and Mastery of Karma

It was not just the Beatles or their guru, the Maharishi Mahesh Yogi; John Lennon's song "Instant Karma," which appeared in a 1992 Nike commercial; or Karma, the telepathic Marvel Comics superheroine from 1980 that popularized the word "karma" in Western society. In his 2005 commencement ad-

dress at Stanford University, Steve Jobs astutely shared with
the graduates that "You have to trust in something—your
gut, destiny, life, karma, whatever." Despite these references,
my sessions with clients clearly reveal that karma is misunder-
stood, partially understood, yet seldom fully understood.

Here are some examples of what I hear: "My karma is my
fate and there's simply nothing I can do about it"; "I heard that
word in the 1960s when my car broke down and my friend
said it happened because of my bad karma"; "Oh #$%$, I
really need to convince the universe to extend me some good
karma credit!" What I particularly notice is the erroneous belief that karma is a punishment for past bad actions or a reward
for good actions. In everyday language, karma can be defined
as "what you send out returns to you." Perform any action, and
the karma meter starts ticking.

The word "karma" first appeared in the ancient *Rig Veda*,
but it is not until the *Upanishads* in 1500 BC that karma is
defined as a universal principle of cause and effect based on
actions. Through the operation of this impersonal causative
principle, the circumstances in your life correspond to the
causes you have set in motion. Whether or not a person believes in karma, whether or not a person is clear on the workings of karma, no one is exempt from its effects. The operation
of cosmic law does not depend upon our belief in it; the truth
just keeps on being the truth.

When karma was introduced as a cornerstone in Eastern
religions, it was conjoined not only with the spiritual principle
of dharma, but also samsara, which is the cycle of life, death,
and rebirth. Both karma, as cause, and dharma, as purpose and
the path to fulfillment of purpose, are inseparably woven into
the fabric of our existence.

"Pardon Me, Have We Met Before?"

Let's say you're sitting in the piano bar of an elegant hotel listening to a terrific jazz combo. Then in walks this man, unseen by you, who sits in close proximity to your table. Suddenly, you sense that you're being stared at. To confirm your feeling, you do your best to inconspicuously turn in the direction from which this energy is emanating. Caught in the act, the man leans toward you and says, "Pardon me, have we met before?" Immediately upon eye contact you experience a jolt of recognition in your solar plexus. Is this connection authentic déjà vu, or is it merely a come-on line to be politely declined, or accepted?

In his book *The Cosmic Game*, Dr. Stanislav Grof, former assistant professor of psychiatry at Johns Hopkins University School of Medicine, writes:

> The most characteristic aspect of past life experience is a convinced feeling that the situation we are facing is not new. . . . This sense of reliving something that one has seen before (déjà vu) or experienced before (déjà vécu) in a previous incarnation is very basic and cannot be analyzed any further. It is comparable to the ability to distinguish in everyday life our memories of events that actually happened from our dreams, daydreams, and fantasies. . . . Past incarnation memories have a similar subjective quality of authenticity and reality. . . . Another interesting feature of past life experiences is that they are often intimately connected with important issues and circumstances in our present life.[1]

My word for the awareness of already knowing a person upon first meeting him or her is "soul-crossing." Individuals gravitate to us and we to them when an agreement was made on the invisible side of life to play the part of parent, child, extended family, friend, lover, spiritual teacher, colleague, casual acquaintance, and even seeming enemy—whatever is required to complete karmic work together.

Whether we are conscious of it or not, we are constantly soul-crossing with individuals with whom we have shared previous lives. With some we will have a lifetime connection, with others it will be temporary or perhaps just a brief encounter. And there are those we can't get away from fast enough. As well, some people may recognize us but we don't recognize them, so the opportunity to connect is missed in this incarnational go-around. There are also individuals we will meet for the first time and with whom we will create a new karmic connection. Obviously, it is to our benefit to pay attention to our gut reaction when first meeting a person.

During readings with clients, I am frequently asked by them about their past life connections to those who have been or are currently impactful in their lives. When, for example, I say to him or her, "Your mother was your child in a previous lifetime," I can't count the number of times they exclaim, "Oh, oh my God! That's exactly what we say to each other!" Sometimes a young person will share the recognition that "It's so clear to me that some of my siblings were with me in a past life, even though they think I'm crazy for saying so."

Get a Second, Third, Fourth . . . Life!

Whenever I facilitate a seminar and ask the participants if there is something they would like to change about their lives, at least 85 percent shoot their hands in the air. So what's preventing them from actualizing their desired changes? A lack of understanding that they themselves are the architects who have built, thought by thought, choice by choice, action by action, the life they are currently living, and that they can remodel their lives by choosing to do so.

This brings to mind what one of my favorite authors, James Allen, writes in his book *As a Man Thinketh*: "They themselves are makers of themselves." His economic word usage is an exclamation point of utmost truth. What encouraging news that regardless of the caravan of karmic patterns that have followed us in this lifetime, we can transform the limiting thoughts, beliefs, opinions, attitudes, attachments, and actions that have held us hostage and begin instead to live from our inborn nature of joy, wisdom, love, creativity, freedom, and intuitive attunement to Spirit, our guides, and ourselves. *This means we can have a new incarnation right within the lifetime we are currently living!*

Before we go any deeper into this subject, I wish to clarify that my writings on reincarnation are not intended to be a complete education on this vast and deeply nuanced subject. I encourage you, if you have not done so already, to study it more thoroughly, including research on the Akashic records. (*Akashic* is a Sanskrit word meaning "outside of time and space.")

Can Reincarnation Be
Biologically Proven?

Dr. Ian Stevenson was a psychiatrist at the University of Virginia School of Medicine for fifty years and founder of its Division of Perceptual Studies, which investigates reincarnation, near-death experience, out-of-body experience, after-death communication, deathbed visions, and altered states of consciousness. It was his 1997 classic, *Where Reincarnation and Biology Intersect*, that caused some hardcore scientists who relied solely on empirical evidence to reconsider the certitude of their position on reincarnation.

During forty years of world travel, Dr. Stevenson investigated three thousand cases involving children who claimed to have had past lives in countries including South Asia, the Shiites of Lebanon and Turkey, West African tribal members, and the American Northwest. Always cautious of fraud and premature conclusions, his impeccable research produced biological evidence that these children had various physical conditions in their lives that were impossible to explain by their environment or heredity, including phobias, illnesses, and birth defects. These same children recounted past lives and experiences in precise detail, many of which Dr. Stevenson corroborated by locating individuals in the places they described who verified that a child had lived and died there and under what circumstances. In some instances, Stevenson took a child into the village or town that she had remembered from a previous life but had not visited in her current life. He found some of these children to be so familiar with the terrain that they actually led him to the homes they had lived in.

"In most cases," he wrote in *Where Reincarnation and Biology Intersect*, "the child continues to talk about the previous life until he or she is about five to seven or eight years old. At this age the memories usually appear to fade. This, however, is a matter difficult to judge, as it seems that some children continue to remember the previous life, but stop speaking about it. They 'go underground,' as it were."[2]

Let me tell you about Demetria, a client of mine. As a child of four living on the Basque sheep camp owned by her immigrant family, nearly every day she insisted that her mother, grandmother, or an extended family member wrap a turban on her head in a very specific way. She also had a habit of placing two chairs about two feet apart, back-to-back, then putting a towel over them to create a tent in which she would silently sit cross-legged for long periods of time. Assuming everyone knew they had lived before, Demetria described to her family in detail previous lives she had in Persia, India, and Morocco. Thinking she was either crazy or lying, her mother and the women elders of their small Basque community agreed that a ritual by a Catholic priest would surely put an end to her nonsense. After three separate rituals of waving incense, sprinkling holy water, and reciting Latin incantations, they gave up.

At the age of ten, while sitting in a doughnut shop with her mother, Demetria noticed that the small jukebox at their table had an additional feature called "Swami Says" which, for five cents, would pop out your fortune. For days thereafter Demetria could not stop writing the word "swami." Determined throughout her younger years to find her spiritual home, at the age of twenty-five she became a Hindu nun for ten years. Referring back to Dr. Stevenson's research, to this day Demetria still has an uncommon, clinically diagnosed phobia for which there is no explanation in this lifetime, a phobia that nearly cost her her life when, as a college student, she jumped from a second-floor balcony.

How about you? Are you strongly drawn to a culture, language, country, or climate that is not your own or have never visited in this lifetime? When you were a child, did you feel that one or both of your parents weren't your "real" parents? Did they ever tell you that as a child you spoke words from another language, or described countries in which you spent a previous life? Is there a historical figure that consumes your interest and has profoundly affected your career or hobbies?

Why should we be interested in reincarnation at all? After all, isn't one lifetime enough to navigate? Dear reader, whatever your beliefs about reincarnation may be, the point is to consciously live your *current lifetime* in such a way that you escort yourself into its ultimate purpose. Consider these words of pioneering transpersonal psychologist Carl Jung: "I could well imagine that I might have lived in former centuries and there encountered questions I was not yet able to answer; that I had been born again because I had not fulfilled the task given to me."[3]

It is we who make repeated rebirths necessary through the choices we make, which in turn determine how many lifetimes it will take to free ourselves from samsara's cycle of birth, death, and rebirth. This is encouraging news because it puts the power precisely where it was originally implanted before taking your first breath: you.

How Spirit's Grace Works with
Your Karma and Dharma

Spirit's unconditional love has graced us with everything we require for living our dharma. During those moments, days, weeks, or even months when we feel we can't get through another minute and we do, that is the operation of grace. When we can't see the light at the end of the tunnel and we do, that is the action of grace. Grace is that ineffable something whispering within, guiding us on our dharmic path.

We have no greater cheerleader on our team than spirit, and it goes to enthusiastic lengths waving its pom-poms as it calls us to "Listen up! Life is on your side." Above all, spirit's grace implanted intuition in our core Self, and it is up to us to cultivate and apply it in our choice making and actions. How often have you said to yourself, "I knew I was supposed to do that! Why didn't I listen?" Or, "I felt I wasn't supposed to go there but I allowed my ego to discount my inner knowing." *Our intuition is meant to be used like smelling salts that we apply to wake up in whatever situation we find ourselves.* Then, even while standing in the lion's lair, we can regain our dharmic footing.

What I'm describing here is a sweet partnership: Spirit provides guidance directly through our intuition, our guides, or a medium, and we, as receptive, willing receivers take action upon the guidance received. Our part is to remove the inner mind-static that would block the flow of this energetic circuitry.

What I wish to etch in your consciousness is that you are never, never alone. While spirit is observing from right within you, it is too respectful of your freedom to interfere. Nor will your guides interfere. So don't waste your time telling spirit or your guides "You *must* tell me what to do!" Instead, practice attuning yourself to spirit's guidance and watch how it mothers you, caresses you, prompts you. Genuine guidance never leaves you with the taste of egoic pride; instead, you are filled with humble gratitude that you were graced with the courage to listen and follow your guidance.

Divine Right Timing: Spirit's Cosmic Clockwork

On numerous occasions I work with clients on something in their lives that has reached its expiration date. Ninety percent of the time they own that it's disconnect time, whether we're talking about marriage, friendship, work, place of residence, even a spiritual path or teacher that has been outgrown. What we struggle with is the ego's need for safety, security, and predictability—the illusion that we can create changeless, solid ground under our feet. So we resist, cling, and grasp that which has outlived its shelf life. We forget that the only changeless thing in our lives is change itself.

Another expression of the stubborn ego is how quickly we are tempted to throw down the gauntlet when something doesn't manifest according to our desired timing. An example is Lettie, a client of mine who requested a reading six months after her husband's passing. Understandably bereft of constant companionship after forty-two years of marriage, she wanted to be rescued from the intensity of her loneliness.

When I shared the guidance that "Now is not the right

time," she fumed, "Then, when *is*? Why doesn't my husband send someone who can fill this void *right now*?" It was a foot-stomping demand that an immediate stop be put to her heart's anguish.

"For many years you've been a wife and a mother," I gently continued. "Now your guides are saying they want to support you in discovering who you are beyond these roles so that you can cultivate more of your individual soul-qualities. These qualities are the treasures that will be recognizable to the new man who will be coming into your life according to Divine right timing."

Lettie was having none of it, and throughout the months that followed drove herself into a nervous breakdown that required her to take antidepressants, all because she was unwilling to trust beyond her desired human timing. Did a new companion eventually enter her life? Yes, a very short six months later.

Trusting spirit's cosmic clockwork inspired me to have some T-shirts made during a time when I had an office in Miami Beach. On the front of the shirt were the words "Get over yourself," and on the back "And get out of your own way." Releasing our overnight delivery expectations and demands harmonizes us with our karma and our dharma. A new level of spiritual maturity takes place in that moment when we stop wasting time listening to mind chatter and instead intuit the "still small voice" forever reverberating in our spirit-soul. Practice my friends, and practice profoundly, for you alone, chapter by chapter, are co-authoring the book of your life with spirit.

Bringing It All Home

The following two exercises are the steps through which you may begin to intuitively receive hints of where some of your present mindsets, heartsets, and habitual patterns originated. The first exercise is intended to sensitize your intuition in preparation for the second exercise.

BUILDING TRUST IN YOUR
FACULTY OF INTUITION

+ In a location where you won't be disturbed, take a comfortable position, letting the weight go from your body while remaining alert.
+ With eyes closed, take a long inhalation through your nose and slowly exhale through your mouth, repeating this three to four times or until your body begins to relax but not fall asleep.
+ With eyes still closed, center your awareness in your solar plexus. Follow your natural rhythm of breathing for a few moments.
+ Next, move your awareness into your heart center and continue breathing.
+ Notice the first thought or question about an aspect of your life that comes into your awareness. Feel more deeply into your heart center and ask a question specifically related to that thought or question.
+ Note the responses your intuition presents. If they are in a critical or judgmental voice, that is not intuition; rather, it's the mind chatter of your inner critic, which

is not to be trusted. If it is from the rational mind, it may argue saying, "Are you kidding? That would never work!" That also is not intuition but rather the protective ego doubting your intuitive faculty. Reach even more profoundly into your heart center and ask the question again, without forcing or projecting a response.

+ With sufficient practice you will be able to decipher the difference between mind chatter and authentic intuitive guidance. You may find it helpful to pause during your day's activities and affirm: "I open my inner ear to the guidance of my intuition, my guides, and spirit."

+ Remember, in addition to practice, practice, practice, do so with loving patience, patience, patience and large doses of compassion.

TAPPING INTO YOUR
CONTINUITY OF EXISTENCE

Apply the first two steps from the preceding practice. Next, place before your intuitive faculty the following questions for uncovering and/or confirming people, places, and events from your past lives.

+ Do you have a profound attraction to a country or countries you've never visited but upon seeing photographs or a news report experience a strong familiarity or feel a deep longing?

+ Have you visited a city or country for the first time and sensed a thousand remembered footsteps under

your feet? Bring such places to mind and feel into
your memory of them.

✦ In childhood, did you remember and perform songs
or dances that you've never learned in this lifetime?
How about speaking words in another language?

✦ Do you have phobias, such as a fear of snakes, even
though you've never had an encounter with a snake
in this lifetime?

✦ Was the religion of your family of origin familiar or
foreign to you?

✦ Is there a spiritual path that you are drawn to but
haven't yet explored?

✦ Do you have a sense of specific professions that feel
familiar to you?

✦ What depth of connection do you feel with your
family members, friends, spiritual teachers? Are you
aware of what karmic circumstances or relationships
you are working on with them?

✦ What life lessons do you sense you brought with you
in your birth suitcase? Which are you consciously
working on? Which are you postponing or ignoring?

Each and every lifetime is unique, both here and in the spirit
world. Every incarnation carries with it the profound impres-
sions made upon the soul's memory. Eventually, when we are
sufficiently evolved, we will recall and be entertained by the
many roles we have played on this great stage called life.

CHAPTER 7

✳

Velcro and Teflon Mindsets:
A Symbiotic Relationship

IN 1948, GEORGE de Mestral, an inventor and rugged mountaineer, went for a brisk hike in the Swiss Alps accompanied by his faithful dog. As was his habit, immediately upon returning home, George began the painstaking task of removing the countless prickly burrs hooked to his clothes and his dog's fur. His ritual was brought to an abrupt halt when, without warning, his inventor's mind was struck by a flash of curiosity. Racing to his workspace, he placed one of the tiny burrs under a microscope. Observing its hundreds of hooks designed to catch on anything with a loop—clothing, shoes, fur, hair—George realized that if he could just figure out how to duplicate this mechanism of nature it could be patented. In 1955 he did just that, and today we earthlings are benefiting from his legacy: Velcro.

Ten years earlier at DuPont's New Jersey facility, chemist Dr. Roy J. Plunkett was working with gases related to Freon refrigerants when he unexpectedly discovered a white, waxy, solid substance with properties resistant to corrosion and high heat. Over the years his discovery produced advancements in aerospace, communications, electronics, and architecture. The first products marketed to the public in 1946 were sold commercially under the trademark Teflon, the most slippery material in existence.

Our Mental Hooks

What is the metaphorical correlation between Velcro, Teflon, and the operating system of the human brain and mind? As Chip and Dan Heath inform us in their book *Made to Stick*, "Your brain hosts a truly staggering number of loops. The more hooks an idea has, the better it will cling to memory."[1]

We human beings dedicate enormous amounts of time and energy creating hooks of beliefs, convictions, theories, concepts, opinions, fantasies, and mind chatter which loop onto our psyche so tightly we are convinced they are infallible truths about ourselves, others, our world, life, and the source of existence. Conversely, intuitive guidance that shakes our foundation, unsolicited words of criticism or advice, bypassed feelings and emotions—all this slips, Teflon-like, right out of our conscious mind.

A Velcro mindset can be a source of heartache and suffering when it hooks us onto a loop of self-denigrating thoughts, which result in unskillful actions. The good news is that through our spiritual practices, reprogramming our subconscious, developing our clairsentience, and by working with our guides and readers we can unhook from what has been looped onto our minds. We can let whatever no longer serves us slide right out of our minds as cleanly as an omelet from a

Teflon frying pan and replace it with self-empowering truths about ourselves, including how so utterly cherished we are by our Creator Source that we have been fully equipped with everything we need to wake up to our authentic self.

Now, just as Velcro hooks both negativity and positivity, Teflon can let negativity *and* positivity slip away from us. How many times do you catch yourself rejecting a sincere compliment, praise for an accomplishment, or your own self-appreciation for the qualities, talents, and skills that accompanied you in your birth suitcase?

Velcro and Teflon mindsets share a symbiotic relationship and it is absolutely within our capacity to make the highest use of both.

The Tortuous Tango of the Conscious and Subconscious Minds

If you've ever danced the tango, seen it in person or in a competition on television, then you have observed, in the footwork alone, the hooks and loops of intense seduction, resistance, and, ultimately, surrender. In dance competitions the tango is precisely choreographed, but on nightclub dance floors each step is improvised, much in the same way life presents us with limitless improvisational opportunities.

The word "tortuous" means "repeatedly swerving in alternate directions," which explains why the tango is a metaphor for our inner dance with life. The choreography goes like this: Our conscious mind has a self-affirming thought. Then the subconscious, swerving toward its negative conditioning, immediately rejects it. The soul's super-consciousness, free of all conditioning, swerves in full surrender to the lead of the self. Without the step of surrender, the tango doesn't happen, it doesn't complete itself. When we restlessly swerve in unskillful mental and emotional directions, we prevent a whole-souled surrender to the lead of the self, and our dance is incomplete.

Interestingly, dancers of the tango have compared its energy to meditation, yoga, relationships, even business management. In meditation, when we become aware of distracting thoughts and arising emotions, we swerve our attention back to the breath and surrender. In yoga, we experience our ability to improvise a posture, and in personal and business relationships we alternate between the roles of leading and following.

The conscious mind is the proverbial "tip of the iceberg" when it comes to our everyday thoughts and interactions with ourselves, others, and life. Dr. Bruce H. Lipton, an internationally recognized cellular biologist and author of *The Biology of Belief*, shared in an interview that "The significant issue here is that we all have two minds that are working in tandem: the conscious and the subconscious. The subconscious mind is a million times more powerful as an information processor than the conscious mind. So, although we think we can control our lives by using our conscious mind, our subconscious programs operate our biology for 95–99 percent of the day, so our lives are actually mostly controlled by our subconscious programs."[2]

When asked how a person can begin to get some control over his subconscious programming, Lipton delivered this good news: "The primary thing is to learn how to practice mindfulness. When you are being mindful and conscious, you are not operating off the prerecorded tapes that typically lead us off-track. Mindfulness practice [developed through meditation] encourages people to get into the practice of being more conscious in their day-to-day lives, of becoming aware. Becoming aware means accessing the behavioral programs in your unconscious mind so that you can change the underlying limiting or self-sabotaging thoughts that don't serve you."[3]

Let's break that down into a more simplified form:

+ **What:** Becoming aware when self-sabotaging tapes are running in your subconscious mind, pressing the stop button, and downloading self-affirming, self-empowering recordings.
+ **Why:** To break through neurotic subconscious mind chatter and begin mindfully living your dharmic purpose of awakening to your true nature.
+ **How:** Through the mindfulness practice of meditation, working with your guides, and cultivating your clairsentience.

Downloading New Programming into the Subconscious Mind

Our subconscious mind has a database of dysfunctional, toxic programs and messages, which, in this lifetime, neuroscientists explain, we pretty much downloaded before reaching the age of six. When a parent tells a child, "You'd better study something less challenging because you're not smart enough for economics," any and all such messages of "not-enoughness" Velcro themselves onto our subconscious mind as literal facts, regardless of what our conscious mind says to contradict them.

New findings in neuroscience provide factual evidence that

we can change how we interpret words and events, which is a good motivator for assuming a greater level of responsibility and discipline in working with our minds. Accepting that we ourselves are both the problem *and the solution* is enormously empowering. That we can stop the relentless, obsessive repetition of mind chatter emanating from the subconscious and regroove our brain circuits is a cause for celebration!

A View from the Invisible Side of Life

When you're gracing the invisible side of life in between each earthly incarnation, your teachers and guides prepare you for the next level of your soul's journey. In a spirit of fun, see yourself sitting with them right now. Then, right before the eye of your soul, imagine that a movie is projected out of the sacred ethers with you in the starring role.

"Precious One," the narrator begins, "this is your life as you lived it in your most recent incarnation." The familiar faces of loved ones, animal companions, enemies, friends, and events, in all of their radiant beauty and dark shadows, pass before you. Only this time, without the ego's intervention, you see them as they really were, not as you filtered them through the narrow lens of "me, myself, and I." You see that those who hurt you were themselves wounded, so compassion and forgiveness now fill your heart. To those who uplifted and supported you, you give a deep bow of gratitude. During those times when you were convinced you were alone and forsaken, you see the spiritual guides and teachers who surrounded and embraced you in unconditional love.

Suddenly, you sense a shadow-like energy overtake the

screen. Moving in for a closer view, you see it contains all the lies you were told by the collective unconscious of societal influences and the ways in which you embodied and lived them. In this moment of compassionate clarity, their illusory nature is revealed and you realize that in truth they had no power except that which you assigned to them. You are shaken into remembrance of how your choices—unconscious and conscious—determined the course of your life in the school of the three-dimensional realm. The movie ends with a revelation of the next stage of your evolutionary progress, and together with your guides, you set the intentions for your next earthly incarnation.

Getting on Track with Your Dharma and Karma

As you learned in chapter 6, your life's dharmic path is based on the karma of past lives and that which you are creating in your current lifetime. A frequent question I place before new students and clients is, "Do you feel you are on track with your dharma?," to which the frequent comeback is, "What track, what dharma?" It's no wonder, because the ego doesn't want you to take credit for anything it didn't initiate or create in your life. The truth is, the conscious and subconscious are afraid that as you realize you are not a self separate from the Whole, they will lose their leading roles in your life. In other words, the ego has nothing to gain from your awakening.

Although your spirit-soul transmits its intuitive guidance, a great percentage of the time it is drowned out by the shrieks of fears, doubts, inadequacies, and other mind chatter of the subconscious mind. Despite how solid, dense, and true they seem, we can dissolve them by claiming and honoring our inherent wholeness, our beauty beyond words, our godliness. One of the greatest tools we have for this is freedom of choice. Through this powerful vehicle we can choose to actualize our innately awakened self, or continue to wallow in our human limitations. As Saint Gregory of Nyssa reminds us, "We are, in a sense, our own parents and we give birth to ourselves by our own free choice of what is good."

Which Wolf Are You Feeding?

To support clients and students in more deeply embodying an understanding of how the karmic law of cause and effect operates in our life choices, I'm fond of telling this story about an old Cherokee who is sharing with his grandson the battle that goes on within human beings.

"My son," he begins, "the battle is between the two wolves inside us all. One is ignorant. It is anger, jealousy, fear, sorrow, shame, greed, arrogance, self-pity, guilt, resentment, inferiority, aggression, false pride, superiority, and ego. The other is wise. It is joy, love, serenity, wisdom, vulnerability, humility, kindness, benevolence, generosity, truth, compassion, and trust."

The grandson, pensive for a moment, turned toward his grandfather and asked, "So, Grandpa, which wolf wins the fight?" The wise grandfather simply replied, "The one that you feed."

I interpret this wolf metaphor similarly to that of Velcro and Teflon relative to the functions of the conscious and sub-conscious mind:

+ What and how are you feeding your powers of mind?
+ Are you allowing old conditioning to continue
  defining who you are and govern your mental
  household, impacting yourself and all those around
  you?
+ Are you empowering your authentic self and
  consciously activating your purpose for being on the
  planet?

If upon raw, honest introspection you conclude that you are feeding the "good wolf," I have a suggestion for you. Right now, on the very spot where you are reading these words, get down on your knees before the altar of your spirit-soul and let out a celebratory howl! Howl with whole-souled abandon, passion, and celebration, for in the continuum of consciousness, the pendulum is swinging in the direction of your evolutionary progress! Let's name this "The Wolf Pose" and create reasons to practice it often!

Reclaiming Your Inborn Wonderment

Even before the moment we arrived on the planet there were those who were already defining their expectations of who and what we would become: our expectant parents. Thanks to today's prenatal technology, parents can know the sex of their child within five weeks after conception, whereas just a short time ago they could only hope that their personal preference would be a reality. As well, it was not so long ago when societal pressures caused a woman to give a sigh of relief when, in the parlance of that time, she "gave her husband a son" so that

"Dudley Jones Jr." would ensure the continuity of the family name.

No consideration was given to how having the same name as his father could deprive the son from having an individual identity. Fortunately, in our postmodern times, science has intervened, revealing that all along it's been the male XY chromosomes that determine the sex of a child. And I can't help but add that married couples now have the opportunity to combine and hyphenate their last name, and women may legally keep their last name, all of which contribute to maintaining one's own unique identity.

Now there is something no scientific discovery has managed to keep out of our lives: parental and societal conditioning. It's a packaged deal that includes inheriting the conditioning our own parents received from their parents, along with their ethics, values, beliefs, opinions, fears, myths, superstitions, and secrets. With no shortage of venues—television, tabloids, social media, beauty contests, advertising, magazines, movies, religious establishments—societal conditioning traffics in defining for us what it means to be successful, valuable, beautiful, handsome, desirable, lovable, employable, acceptable, respectable, upstanding, and moral.

Universally, the collective consciousness of religious, political, and educational institutions impose their values in order to control new generations by maintaining the status quo. For example, how many people do you know who would like to see a return to the "ideal" family values depicted in 1950s television programs like *Father Knows Best*, *The Donna Reed Show*, or *Leave It to Beaver*? Never mind that denial and family secrets lurked everywhere, beginning with the twin beds slept in by the parents who told their children they were delivered by a stork, that they were first "a twinkle in their mommy's eye."

I know of no spirit-soul who, preparing for their re-appearance on the planet, measures its self-worth by the size of its future hips or biceps, not to mention other physical characteristics. What we most long to accompany us in our birth suitcase is our own self-love, self-respect, self-acceptance, self-empowerment. Indeed, no matter how many lifetimes we've had, each time we reenter this three-dimensional world we arrive with fresh eyes of wonder and innocence. Just look into the eyes of a baby in a new environment and you will see that they are filled with wonder as they drink in the scenery, the sounds, the ways life reaches in and touches their inner-most being.

Toward the end of his life Albert Einstein memorably said, "I have been thinking the whole of my life that I would demystify the universe. But what has happened is just the con-trary. The deeper I went into existence, the more the mystery deepened. I am dying full of wonder, I am dying in wonder." Now this was not the result of knowledge he discovered in a test tube or when formulating his mind-boggling equations; it resulted from the wisdom he garnered from deep within his own spirit. Before Einstein died someone asked him, "If you were reborn, I'm sure you would like to become a great physicist and mathematician once again." He must have stunned his questioner with his response: "If another oppor-tunity is given to me, rather than being a physicist I would like to become a plumber. Fame, prestige, research—nothing coming my way, so that I could have a deeper communion with existence."

Let me ask you a few questions: When was the last time

your own eyes lit up in wonder? Can you remember a time when you allowed your creative energy to fill you with inspiration, to guide you to the fulfillment of your dreams? What about creating or expressing something without the fear of others' opinions? How frequently do you laugh so genuinely that it bubbles up from the very core of your being?

Wonderment, dear friends, is a state of consciousness that is our birthright; therefore it is available to us at all ages and stages of life. If you want life's mysteries to open up for you, enter a state of wonder.

How to Become Your Own Provocateur

In his extraordinary book *Cosmos*, Carl Sagan wrote: "Every one of us is, in the cosmic perspective, precious. If a human disagrees with you, let him live. In a hundred billion galaxies, you will not find another."[4] And, "The nitrogen in our DNA, the calcium in our teeth, the iron in our blood, the carbon in our apple pies were made in the interiors of collapsing stars. We are made of starstuff."[5]

It's a conundrum that we human beings are more willing to risk losing our lives going to the moon—as some indeed have—than to risk what can be discovered by exploring the vast universe within us. Do you find it as perplexing as I do that we'd rather take selfies and spend endless hours Velcroed to electronics while ignoring the fact that every enlightened sage, saint, savant, and swami has instructed us to use the time we have on the planet to "Know thyself"?

The word "provoke" comes from late Middle English meaning to invoke or summon, and from the Latin *provocare*, which means "to challenge." A provocateur is a person who knows what they must do to provoke themselves to get back on their dharmic track, who courageously faces all that stands in their way of claiming their original Self.

You'll note I chose the adjective "courageously" rather than "fearlessly." A provocateur isn't an individual who feels no fear. It's a matter of him or her being courageous enough to move closer to fear with respect and openness, to silently stand in it long enough to discover its empty, illusory nature. *Once standing in the face of your deepest fears, you realize the only power they have over you is that which you give them.* And during those times when we're stuck and can't be our own provocateurs, we can rely on our spiritual teachers and guides to give us a kick-start.

As your willingness increases to be your own provocateur, you will notice that scrambling after unnecessary necessities, fruitless activities, and empty entertainment begins to slide, Teflon-like, off your to-do list. Your priorities become re-arranged and no longer will you continue to let yourself be distracted from your distractions by new distractions. The voice of your inner restlessness, anxiety, and resistance begins to lower its volume and eventually fade into the nothingness out of which it came.

No matter what it takes to birth the authentic self, a spiritual warrior never, ever gives up on him- or herself. And that, dear one, is why it is such a joy for me to midwife such a birthing by transmitting from the invisible side of life the healing, comforting, transforming messages of guides, loved ones, and even so-called enemies that contribute to the demystification and clearing away of blockages, hindrances, the seemingly impassable obstacles to fulfilling one's karma and dharma.

Then, at last, when you gaze into the mystical mirror, your true reflection is fully revealed.

Bringing It All Home

EXCAVATING THE TREASURE OF SELF

Complete the sentences below with the first responses that come to you. Don't overthink them or the ego will attempt to edit your stream-of-consciousness writing. There are quite a few questions, so to avoid creating stress, consider dividing your writing session into shifts. After you finish answering the questions put your writing aside, and when you feel ready proceed to the second practice.

1. Overall, my life is . . .
2. And that makes me feel . . .
3. Is this accurate, true?
4. Are my values, goals, and dreams authentically my own?
5. What is my heart telling me beyond the contents of my mind?
6. Do I trust Life?
7. Do I trust my clairsentience and my guides?
8. Do I put mine and their guidance into practice?
9. What is in my bag of tricks for bypassing intuitive guidance I prefer to ignore?
10. Am I conscious of my motives, intentions?
11. In what areas do I need my own forgiveness?
12. In what areas do I need to forgive others?
13. Whose forgiveness do I need?

14. What is my relationship to the Ineffable, Unnameable Creator Source?

15. Do I feel aligned with my dharma?

AWAKENING YOUR SELF-REMEMBRANCE

Our guides, readers, and teachers are our compassionate, generous, grace-giving cheerleaders, and our spiritual practices and studies are our technologies for awakening. But only we ourselves can do the work of waking up to our true nature. In other words, we alone look *for* ourselves *within* ourselves, which is the purpose of the following exercise and meditation.

+ Find a quiet spot where you won't be disturbed for at least twenty minutes. Sitting comfortably and gently closing your eyes, become present to yourself as you focus your energy in your heart center.

+ Feel into your wide-open spaciousness. Inwardly place yourself on the lap of spirit, surrounded by the loving, energetic presence of your guides.

+ Rest your attention on your breath, relaxing as you inhale and exhale for several moments. Whatever thoughts enter your mind, make no effort to chase them away; simply observe them and let them go by like clouds moving through the sky. If any of them hook you, simply bring your attention back to your breath.

+ Now place these questions, one at a time, before your inner self: "Who am I?" "What is the purpose for which I was born?" Whether answers come in this moment or not, remember that these are open-ended questions to which answers continuously evolve in concert with your evolutionary progress.

✦ Next, go to a room where you have a mirror and can see yourself up close. Quietly stand or sit, looking at the person looking back at you. How does what you *see* connect to what you *feel* when responding to the question "Who am I?" Do you sense an "un-pin-down-able" quality of self—an energy essence that simply is, beyond personality, mind, and body? Do you feel a connection to being the "starstuff," the molecules of spirit out of which you are made? Remember, the membrane between you, the other side, and spirit is far thinner than you realize.

✦ Whether or not you feel the godliness of your essence, look directly into your eyes and say, "Right now I may not know precisely who you are, but I am on my way to knowing your true identity and living the dharma and karma of this incarnation. Thank you for being me."

After some days have elapsed, go back and reread your answers to the questions in this exercise and meditation. Would you revise any of your answers based on what you are learning and practicing? Every now and then you may want to check in with yourself and see how your subconscious is clarifying, how you are cultivating an intimate self-acquaintance with yourself.

CHAPTER 8

Looking at Death
with Seeing Eyes

WHILE WRITING THIS chapter, a client who had come to see me following the death of her beloved husband came into my awareness. Clarissa was in her early forties at the time of Matthew's passing and had become entangled in a vigorous legal struggle over his estate with his children from a previous marriage, causing her to be certain she was going to lose everything.

"This will all be resolved in a favorable manner," spirit instructed me to tell her. She did not hesitate to share her assessment that neither spirit's message nor I had substantially relieved her angst, that the essence of the message was too vague since it lacked the important "how and when" details she required to put her mind at ease.

Imagine my surprise when, a few weeks later, Clarissa gave me a call to share that she had been hit by a car. She recounted how, immediately after vacating her physical body, her awareness was riveted upon the presence of an angel at her side and how both she and the angel were enveloped in luminous rays of light. As her energy began recalibrating to accommodate her new reality, she realized that the angel was her husband, just as he had looked as a young man. He then said to her, "You are going to survive and return to the world you think you left behind. And when you do, everything is going to work out just fine," upon which she reentered her physical body. It was then that the attending physician standing at her ICU bedside told her that the paramedics who picked her up from the street, finding no vital signs, administered CPR and rushed her to the emergency room.

Clarissa's journey had a happy ending. She and Emily, the daughter she and her husband had brought into the world, became grateful beneficiaries of Matthew's estate. And I became the grateful beneficiary of witnessing spirit's outstretched hand of unceasing grace that is ever upon each of our lives.

I count among my greatest blessings in life the joy that comes from assisting clients to realize that their individual spirit-soul not only continues its unique journey after leaving the earthly realm, but also that they may take on the role of guardian angel, as did Clarissa's husband, Matthew, which is something I learned when I was quite young through my own near-death experience.

At the age of ten, I was totally into fishing. On any given sunny Saturday morning, fishing gear in hand, off I'd go to the local pier. It was pure magic peering into the depths of a world so mysterious and vastly populated with thousands of varieties of plants, fishes, and, who knows—maybe even buried treasure!

I figured other boys in my neighborhood would feel likewise, so I began inviting them to come along. Little did I know that one of them was a bully. Ironically nicknamed Buddy, he did not hesitate to unleash his rants upon me. One day, having had quite enough and assuming my height would overpower his girth, I verbally retaliated. That's also the day I learned that one of the pier's wooden railings was loose. One heave-ho from Buddy and I fell into eight feet of water!

Over and over again my head kept banging against a bulging rock. I then heard my inner voice say, "I just died!" My master guide instantly appeared at my side. "Just temporarily," he nonchalantly advised. Elaborating in sparse language, he said, "It's not yet your karmic moment to die." Then, just as spontaneously as he appeared—poof! He disappeared. All at once I felt someone grab my body, pick me up, and place me on the dry sandy shore. Upon looking up, I saw the blondest hair I'd ever seen and eyes so blue I was sure I was being rescued by an angel. As I more fully reentered the physical realm, I realized there was a lifeguard standing over me applying some sort of technique to make me breathe. "The paramedics are here now," he said, endeavoring to comfort me as he stepped aside. While the paramedics were bandaging my head, I asked the lifeguard, "I want to say thank you—where is the man who brought me to shore?"

"There was no one with you when I saw you through my binoculars or when I got to your side. You hit your head so hard it probably caused you to hallucinate."

Obviously, my angel didn't hang around long enough to receive my gratitude. But that night he came to me in the dream state and I was able tell him how grateful I was, and how because of him I was reminded that I am always accompanied by invisible companions keeping watch over me. He just smiled as his form slowly dissolved into the ethers from which it came, those otherworldly blue eyes the last vestige of his being that I saw but will never forget.

I hope that by sharing Clarissa's and my personal stories you can see that each of us has guardian angels assigned to support us throughout our earthly walk. And we don't have to rely on a religious source to define their job description. Instead, we can turn to that most trusted of human resources—the dictionary. The *American Heritage Dictionary* offers us this definition: "Angel: A guardian spirit or guiding influence," and *Webster's Revised Unabridged Dictionary* has this: "Angel: A spiritual, celestial being, superior to man in power and intelligence. In the Scriptures the angels appear as God's messengers."

Death, the Great Illusion

If you were to ask me which aspect of human existence towers above all others, it would unequivocally be that of death. Indeed, death holds an incomparable place in the lives of people within every culture and society. If we are honest, which of us has not asked ourselves, "When will the moment of my death come; how will I die; and, where will I go?" Living so intimately with ourselves as we do, it can feel like a personal affront that we are not privy to the answers! Alas, none of us arrives on the planet stamped with a shelf life or "best used by November 21, 2022." We can, however, read in the autobiographies and biographies of some yogis, mystics, saints, sages, and shamans whose spiritual advancement was so great that they not only intuitively knew the moment of their death, they also were able to consciously exit the physical form.

Now to alleviate any sense of "I don't see myself arriving at that state of consciousness in this lifetime," be encouraged by the fact that even great spiritual masters shutter when breaking the bond of attachment to the physical form, as was pointed out by the great yogi Patanjali in his *Yoga Sutras*, 11:9: "Attachment to bodily residence, springing up of its own nature, is present in slight degree even in great saints." We also find a related reference in the gospel of Luke, 22:42, which describes one of Jesus's visits to the Mount of Olives with his disciples, only this time with a significant difference. Knowing the time of his death was approaching, Jesus wanted to sequester himself to begin preparing his consciousness for this transition. Stepping away from his disciples, he poured out his heart to spirit in prayer saying, "Father, if you are willing, remove this cup from me; yet not my will, but yours be done."

Attachment to our physical form, as Patanjali stated, "springs up of its own nature." In other words, it's organic to the human condition. When death opens the door of our physical captivity, we become like a caged bird that is not so eager to exit and fly to a realm that is no longer familiar. Although graphic descriptions by those who have glimpsed the ineffable beauties of the other side during a near-death experience extend to us a comforting grace, even this doesn't banish the natural shutter of hesitation to leave the familiar confines of our bodily habitat.

Various scientific disciplines continue to examine and re-examine death, causing it to be defined and redefined. These efforts are further complicated by the definition of when life begins. Is it at the time of conception, at some stage of embryonic development, upon taking that first breath after exiting the birth canal? With the exception of religious doctrines—which aren't necessarily in agreement—the precise moment when life begins remains a mysterious, open-ended question, and so is it true of death.

There was a time when death was defined by cardiac arrest, the cessation of breathing, or a comatose state. However, advancements in medical technology such as CPR and life support systems have literally brought individuals back from clinical death (not to mention the attempt to reach immortality through cryogenics). That being said, the purpose of this book is not to debate contemporary philosophical, scientific, religious, or moral theories about death. Rather, my intention is threefold: to expand society's collective understanding that the transition into the finer dimension of living is a joyously liberating one; to offer human hearts the comfort of knowing we have an unbroken connection to loved ones who have made that transition; and how our continuity of consciousness beyond the third dimension announces that death is the greatest illusion, for it is only by dying that we continue living.

The Invisible Self

Upon considering the amount of time and energy devoted to eating, digesting, eliminating, beautifying, exercising, resting, transporting, and hygienically caring for the physical body, it becomes obvious why we are so fiercely attached to it, why it is more real to us than the formless self, which is not visible to our external eyesight. Add that to our mental and emotional attachments and we lose sight of the true self that is traveling within us: our spirit-soul. It is this unseen self that is the reality of our existence. Simply because we cannot see its luminous life force vibrating within us does not mean that it is nonexistent.

I take the liberty of speaking for humanity in general when saying that it is equally challenging for us to recognize how the ego's fear of losing its sense of being a self separate from the Whole causes us—as the idiom goes—"to fight for dear life" against life's seemingly greatest opponent: death. In my work with clients who were given a prognosis of a few months to live, with the uttermost compassion I've observed natural death-related emotions—fear, sadness, anger, remorse, guilt, denial—overtake them in the face of this daunting news. And yet, sitting with dear ones in their last moments, when that last breath comes, without exception it has been my blessing to witness "the peace that surpasseth all understanding" enfold them in a mantle of unconditional love. And I tell you there have been no exceptions to this—whether the individual was devoutly religious, nontheistic, agnostic, or atheistic. If there is any grace I can offer you, it is that you are as cherished by our Creator Source as is any saint, avatar, sage, or enlightened being, and in that moment of transition into the spirit world, your arrival is as joyously celebrated as is their own.

Having communicated with individuals on the other side for most of my life, and knowing that transitioning to the other side is filled with unspeakable bliss, I assure you that we human beings are fully capable of embracing life's greatest paradox: we must die so that we may live.

There Are Only Beginnings

Since ancient times human birth has been universally celebrated through cultural, social, and spiritual rituals, and numerous are the worldwide traditions that annually honor a person's birthday. Likewise, on the yearly anniversary of a loved one's death, we express our loving remembrance of him

or her in ceremonies unique to our cultural or personal observances. These sacred rituals are rooted in an inherent knowing,
deep within the human spirit, that each birth and rebirth in
the physical realm and astral realm announce new beginnings
in our soul's ever-evolving journey.

Several months out of the year I live in Mexico, a land dear
to my heart. Come late October there is a stirring in my spirit
as the annual celebration venerating deceased loved ones that
dates back some 2,500 to 3,000 years ago approaches—*Día de
los Muertos*. On October 31, All Hallows' Eve, children create a
home altar and invite the spirits of their deceased siblings to return to their family dwelling for a visit. On November 1 adults
create an altar and invite the spirits of adult family members
who died to visit. Then, on November 2, family and friends
visit the cemeteries and create elaborate altars at the gravesides
of their loved ones. Toys and photographs are set out on the
graves of children. On the graves of adults you will see their
favorite foods and beverages. Marigolds adorn their photos
and sugar skulls, incense, decorations, and other traditional
items are lovingly placed. While their favorite songs are sung
to the strumming of guitars, tears intermingled with joy and
sadness are shed. Stories are told and toasts are made as prayers
and soft laughter echo throughout the cemetery. I consider it
a privilege to take part in these precious festivities, which, as
you may know, are also celebrated by Mexicans living in the
United States.

Research any country and you can read about each one's
unique rituals for honoring deceased loved ones. Many of my
international clients have shared with me how they celebrate
in their respective countries. For example, in Brazil, *Dia
de Finados* is a holiday during which many Brazilians visit

cemeteries and churches. In Spain, loved ones are honored at festivals and parades, which end at cemeteries where prayers are offered at their grave sites. Day of the Skulls is celebrated on May 5 in Bolivia, and in Haiti voodoo traditions mix in Roman Catholic observances. In the Philippines, All Saints' Day is celebrated, while the Chinese celebrate Ghost Month.

Families and friends who participate in these festivities find great comfort in sharing their love-offerings with loved ones. And although they are separated by physical time and space, they tangibly experience that there is no distance between their souls.

The Shifting Perceptions of Death and Dying

Thanatology, the scientific study of death, including its psychological and social aspects, began in 1903 with Russian microbiologist Élie Metchnikoff. Although he compassionately called for the creation of a scientific discipline devoted to assisting individuals facing death in softening their fears, he was too far ahead of his time, evidenced by the fact that few medical school educators supported his theories. His vision didn't materialize until after World War II, when the horrific loss of so many soldiers motivated scientific researchers to begin directing their attention to the psychological impact of death on the dying and the bereaved.

Then, in 1959, a far-reaching breakthrough occurred when Herman Feifel, an American psychologist, edited a volume of essays titled *The Meaning of Death*, with contributions from psychiatrist Carl Jung, theologian Paul Tillich, and philoso-

pher Herbert Marcuse, finally breaking the taboo of the scientific study of death and the treatment of dying persons and
the bereaved. To underscore our societal resistance to dealing
with the subject of death, it has been documented that more
material on thanatology became available in the five years following Feifel's book than in the previous one hundred years!
It's no wonder that he is considered the father of the modern
death movement.[1]

It was Feifel's pioneering work that inspired Dr. Elisabeth
Kübler-Ross, a Swiss psychiatrist, to conduct her own research
and write her 1969 international bestselling book, *On Death
and Dying*, which outlines the five stages that dying persons
experience. Her groundbreaking work revolutionized how individuals in the dying process were treated and tremendously
shifted our Western tendency to avoid explicitly discussing
death, preferring instead to use euphemistic terms such as "bit
the dust," "kicked the bucket," "breathed his last," "cashed
in her chips," "gave up the ghost," "is pushing up daisies."
Interestingly, when reading about Kübler-Ross's life, I learned
that in the late 1970s she was known to have an interest in
mediumship as a way of communicating with deceased loved
ones. Her research in the field of parapsychology included how
individuals in the dying process described sensations such as
floating out of their bodies and having visions of a previously
deceased loved one. Kübler-Ross delved deeply into researching these experiences, resulting in her conviction that death
is not an end in itself but rather a transition into another
dimension of living.

One of Kübler-Ross's greatest legacies to humanity occurred in 1972 when she testified at the first national hearings
of the US Senate's Special Committee on Aging. In her testi-

mony she boldly informed its members that "We live in a very particular death-denying society. We isolate both the dying and the old, and it serves a purpose. They are reminders of our own mortality. We should not institutionalize people. We can give families more help with home care and visiting nurses, giving the families and patients the spiritual, emotional, and financial help in order to facilitate the final care at home."[2]

The Sacred Solitariness of the Dying Process

Being in the presence of our dying loved ones enables us to witness the outer appearance of their death, but not the *inner experience* taking place at the very core of their consciousness. Even if they are able to verbalize some of what is occurring, we cannot enter the interiority, the profound intimacy of the sacred sojourn that is solitarily their own. Nevertheless, we owe a debt of gratitude to those who have built upon Metchnikoff's pioneering work for the tremendous strides that have been made in increasing our understanding of the dying process. Equally valuable is how their work provides us the solace of knowing that we, just like our departed loved ones, will be accompanied by an assisting grace as we navigate our exit from the physical form and transition into our new dimension of living on the invisible side of life.

Many are the individuals who stand upon the broad shoulders of Elisabeth Kübler-Ross's revolutionary work of caring for individuals in the dying process. Outstanding among them is Kathleen Dowling Singh, PhD, a transpersonal psychologist, hospice worker, and worldwide lecturer. It is considered that her groundbreaking book *The Grace in Dying* expands the work of Kübler-Ross to include a dying person's final stages of spiritual and psychological transformation. Sitting at the bedsides of countless patients who related to her the stages through which they were passing as death announced its approach, Dr. Singh named this process the "Nearing Death Experience," which she defines as "an apparently universal process marked primarily by the dissolution of the body and the separate sense of self and the ascendancy of spirit. The Nearing Death Experience occurs from several weeks to several days, even hours or minutes before death. This unique psycho-spiritual process appears to be a sequence of increasingly higher or deeper levels of consciousness, each more enveloping that the next, through which each of us passes as we complete our experience in the human body. The Nearing Death Experience is characterized by certain subtle signals or 'qualities' that, when observed, begin to define its parameters, to indicate that the dying person has entered a significant and transforming field of experience."[3]

The Near-Death Experience

During my research for this chapter, I was fascinated to learn that there are reports of near-death experiences dating back to the Ice Age. Near-death experiences (NDEs) have appeared in folklore and in religious writings from throughout the world including Native America, Tibet, Japan, Micronesia, Egypt, China, India, Australia, Europe, and the United States.

Kenneth Ring, PhD, interviewed 102 near-death survivors while conducting research for his book *Life at Death*. Among the individuals who shared their journey with him were not only those who returned to life after being pronounced clinically dead, but also persons who had attempted suicide. I share here some of Ring's findings on the commonalities within the near-death experience, more of which can be found on his official website included in the Notes section for chapter 8.

+ Those cases who came closest to death, or were clinically dead, just as Moody's cases reported, told of being outside of their bodies, of moving through a void or dark tunnel toward a luminous light, of meeting with departed relatives and friends, of having a feeling of great comfort and bliss and of being surrounded by compassionate love, a feeling so beautiful they longed to remain, and when they returned to the "earthly" realm, they were affected by this feeling the rest of their lives.

+ No one type of person was especially likely to have this experience. It cut across race, gender, age, education, marital status, and social class.

+ Regardless of their prior attitudes—whether skeptical or deeply religious—and regardless of the many variations in religious beliefs and degrees of skepticism from tolerant disbelief to outspoken atheism—most of these people were convinced that they had been in the presence of some supreme and loving power and had had a glimpse of a life yet to come.

+ Based on the information of those who had reported such incidents, the moment of death was often one of unparalleled beauty, peace, and comfort—a feeling of total love and total acceptance. This was possible even for those involved in horrible accidents in which

they suffered very serious injuries. Dr. Ring found
there was a tremendous comfort potential in this
information for people who were facing death.[4]

The Heart Chakra: A Broadcasting
and Receiving Station

My sole purpose as a medium is to be a vehicle of support to
clients and students, encouraging them to be open and accepting of their own inherent capacity to communicate with those
in the spirit world. Above all, I do my best to facilitate their
discovery and actualization of this ability.

Where communicating with departed loved ones is concerned, here are the three most commonly asked questions I
get from clients and students:

1. How can I send my thoughts and feelings to loved
   ones beyond random, hit-or-miss efforts?
2. How can I receive messages sent to me from my
   departed loved ones?
3. How can I contact loved ones who have already
   reincarnated in the three-dimensional realm?

You will be happy to know that your messages to loved ones
can be broadcasted from the heart chakra, and that you can
receive their messages at that same center point of intuition.
The entire chakra system is, quite literally, a masterpiece of the
Divine's creation. Chakras are known as "wheels" in Sanskrit,
which are points of energy in the subtle astral body that circu-
late the life force known as *prana*, or *chi*. For our current pur-

pose, our focus will be on the heart or *anahata* chakra, which is located in the center of the breastbone and is composed of very subtle yet powerful energy. Do not be fooled by the seeming simplicity of the instructions that follow, because for them to fulfill their purpose our familiar friend, mind chatter, has to take a hike. Keep in mind that this technique requires disciplined practice. As well, results may come days later while you're standing at the kitchen sink or jogging in the park. But when they do arrive, you will have absolutely no doubt about their authenticity.

+ Locate yourself in a quiet spot where you will not be interrupted for at least twenty minutes. Turn off all your electronic gizmos so they won't interrupt or distract you. Take a seated position as you would when sitting in meditation posture.
+ Begin by becoming centered through a brief meditation, prayer, chant, or all three. Once you feel an energy of stillness enter your awareness, move to the next step.
+ Visualize the loved one to whom you wish to send a message or from whom you wish to receive a message. You may choose to focus on their appearance during a special time in your connection or when they were healthy, vibrant, and happy.
+ Focus your awareness in the heart chakra, located in the center of the breastbone, and rest there for a few minutes. As a means of better locating this chakra, you may place your fingers directly on the center of your breastbone, press gently, then remove your hand while maintaining your awareness at that spot.

+ *To send a message:* Begin by affectionately, respectfully
  greeting your loved one by name as you visualize
  him/her in your inner eye. Convey your message in
  the language of your heart, remaining centered in
  your heart chakra.
+ *To receive a message:* Visualize your loved one and
  address him/her by name. In language that emerges
  from your deepest self say, for example, "Miriam,
  my heart is open and receptive to any message you
  wish to convey to me. My spirit-soul is completely
  available to our dharma and karma as we continue to
  love each other and honor our soul-agreement."
+ *To communicate with a loved one reincarnated in the
  third dimension:* You may, of course, have a session
  with a medium to support your efforts; however,
  there is no stronger magnetic pull of one heart to
  another than the karmic intensity of the relationship
  you share. Apply the same steps outlined in the
  "To send a message" step, and do so with patience,
  patience, patience. You may also apply the "To
  receive a message" step to open yourself to their
  response.
+ Do not force or demand anything. Let your motive
  be simply one of unconditional love and trust in the
  agreements made while you were last together on the
  other side or on earthly terrain.
+ After you feel complete, remain centered for a few
  moments and close with a prayer of gratitude.

Don't be surprised if your loved one shows up in your dreams,
or if a mutual friend or relative gives you a call and brings up

their name. Again, do not be demanding or look for signs or you might block communication with your mental static. After all, your dear one also must prepare in consciousness and communicate according to Divine right timing. Trust. Then trust some more. Let your heart be comforted by the fact that whether your loved ones are inhabiting the astral realm or have already reincarnated, their spirits also know the eternality of the Divine Love you share, independent of your respective locations.

Bringing It All Home

Learning to relate to death of the physical form in a more accepting manner is one of the most tremendously loving, compassionate gifts we can give ourselves. Not only do we become a beneficiary of a healthy, realistic relationship with death, it also prepares us to offer a more heart-centered support to loved ones in the process of dying, as well as to grieving family and friends who have lost a dear one.

The questions that follow are offered with the intention to assist you in becoming more intimately acquainted with your current relationship to death. They have been created from the wide spectrum of questions, confusions, arguments, pain, joys, and experiences that have been presented to me in over fifty years of client sessions. Although not all of the questions may apply to you, were you to speculate how you would respond, it just might open a door of insight. The questions are grouped into three aspects of relating to death: emotional, ethical, and spiritual.

Due to the highly sensitive nature of the subject of death,

some of the questions may stir up feelings you may first want to process before proceeding, so answer each question only when you feel ready to do so. Above all, be compassionate and patient with yourself should you bump into emotions not previously experienced. Don't hesitate to cry or allow the fullness of your feelings to express. And remember, at any point you can turn to your spirit guides for their loving support.

EMOTIONAL RELATIONSHIP TO DEATH

1. When you were a child, was it acceptable to discuss death in your family? Did your parents themselves explain death to you? If not, from whom and under what circumstances did you first learn of it?
2. To the best of your recollection, at what age did you have your first direct encounter with the death of a loved one or pet? How did you support yourself or how were you supported through the experience?
3. In retrospect, when dealing with the death of a loved one, is there anything you would have changed if you could have?
4. At this point in your life, is there a specific death that has most impacted you? Whose was it and how did you process your feelings of loss and grief, or the lack of feeling loss or grief?
5. What is the most challenging aspect of death for you to deal with?
6. Would you be comfortable having an intimate conversation with a dying person?
7. Are you afraid of death itself, or more afraid of how you will die?

8. Do you wish you knew the time of your death?

9. Have you completed a Healthcare Directive describing whether you do or don't want to be placed on life support or receive extraordinary measures? Have you assigned power of attorney to someone you trust will execute your wishes, even if they aren't a family member?

10. Have you created a will or living trust in the event of your death? Have you discussed with your spouse/ partner/children/or in the absence of them a friend, how you wish your remains to be handled? What kind of funeral or memorial you would like?

11. If you want to be cremated, have you indicated where you would like your ashes to be spread or to whom they would be given?

12. Have you ever created your own obituary—mentally or in writing? Do you find the very thought of it unappealing, or interesting?

13. How long do you expect your spouse or partner to wait before they move on with their life after your death? Have you discussed this with him or her?

14. Do you have a "bucket list"? If not, would you consider creating one? If so, have you begun checking off any items?

ETHICAL RELATIONSHIP TO DEATH

1. Do you believe that dying people should be told that they are dying? If not, why not?

2. Are there any circumstances under which you feel suicide is justified?

3. Do you know anyone who has committed suicide? What was your reaction?

4. What are your views on physician-assisted euthanasia? If it appeared on a ballot where you live, would you vote for or against it? Why or why not?

5. If you were told by your doctor that you had only three months to live and physician-assisted euthanasia were legal in your state, would you consider it?

6. If you were experiencing a physically excruciating dying process, would you request physician-assisted euthanasia if it were legal where you live?

SPIRITUAL RELATIONSHIP TO DEATH

1. How does the culture or religion you were born into deal with death? Do you hold their beliefs to be true, or do you question any of them? Do you feel afraid or uncomfortable seeking answers beyond what they offer?

2. How does your current spiritual path impact your relationship to death? How does it inform your understanding of the afterlife, reincarnation, what happens to pets when they die?

3. Have you researched death or death-related subjects such as reincarnation, near-death experiences, etc., in books, a seminar, or a class in thanatology?

4. While in the presence of a dying loved one, did he/she ever share with you that they were having or had a visitor from the other side? Did you believe it? How did it affect you?

5. Have you ever known someone who has had a near-death experience? Did you believe the details as they were described to you? What was your reaction?

6. Are there any loved ones in your life who have died and with whom you would like to make amends, send and/or receive a message from? Would you be likely to apply the technique described in this chapter?

7. How has the death of a loved one changed you?

8. If you could choose how you were going to die, what would that look like?

9. In spite of the natural sadness upon the loss of a loved one, can you also feel how their release from the physical body would give them tremendous freedom?

10. Do you believe that the souls of your departed loved ones can or do visit you?

11. Has a deceased loved one ever visited you in the dream state? How did this impact you?

12. In what ways do you think your life would be different if you were able to communicate with those who are watching over you from the spirit world?

13. Are you open to continuing a relationship with a loved one who has passed on?

14. Considering that angels are meant to guide and support us during our earthly walk, in what areas of your life would you ask for their assistance?

15. What spiritual practices in your life would bring you into a state of consciousness that would enable you to receive messages from your angelic guides?

CHAPTER 9

The Intuitive Intelligence
of the Heart

RAY KURZWEIL, a respected futurist and bestselling author, writes in his book *How to Create a Mind*: "Sometimes people think that emotion and art are sort of sideshows to human intelligence and the real essence of intelligence is thinking logically. If that were true, computers are already smarter than we are because they're much better at logical thinking than we are. Intelligence actually involves things like being funny, being sexy, or expressing a loving sentiment, maybe in a poem or in a musical piece. That's what today humans are still better at than machines."[1]

Mr. Kurzweil points out a common misunderstanding we have about the difference between the cognitive intellect of the mind and the intuitive intelligence of the heart. To be *intellectual* is an achievement of knowledge learned and stored in the mind which, when applied to things such as scientific theories, innovative architectural designs, complex business decisions, technological advances, shows off the intellect as the awesomely brilliant instrument that it is. In contrast, to be *intelligent* is not something we achieve, because intelligence is an innate quality within the consciousness of every human being, requiring only that it be applied. My clients, Frank and Jerome, are perfect examples.

Frank, a high-achieving lawyer, possesses a very analytical mind that doesn't turn off simply by walking out of the courtroom. His husband, Jerome, a successful international interior designer, is a perfect heart-complement to Frank. Having traveled frequently to the Central American paradise of Belize, they tossed about the possibility of moving there someday and opening a charter fishing business, a sport to which they devote their leisure time. Things came to a standstill, however, when Frank announced how, "logically speaking," it just wouldn't work, which is what led to their making an appointment for a session.

After sharing the pros and cons of uprooting themselves from New York and moving to Belize, Frank, especially, was not prepared for the seeming "illogic" of spirit's guidance: "Why are you dreaming about your intention instead of doing something about it?" This led to an immediate outbreak of Frank's mind chatter enumerating the reasons why they could not move forward at this time. To support them in becoming more objective and concrete, I gave Jerome the assignment to design the fishing resort and Frank to draw up a business plan, "just for the fun of it," which both men agreed to do.

During our next session, Frank introduced a most unexpected factor into the equation: He and Jerome were about to become parents. Frank's sister, Emily, was informed by her physician that she was in the advanced stages of breast cancer with a prognosis of just weeks remaining to her life. When breaking this news to Frank and Jerome, she informed them that when she and her husband created their living trust, it included that should anything happen to them, Frank was entrusted with the raising of their twins, Brent and Ryan. Sadly, Emily's husband had died two years earlier when the boys were just four years old.

Frank and Jerome loved Brent and Ryan very much and frequently took them fishing on the weekends. Nevertheless, parenthood was not on their radar and both were stunned with the reality that they would soon be a family of four, which, exactly six weeks after their conversation with Emily, did fulfill itself.

Assuming that Frank and Jerome were busily adjusting to their new life and still grieving the loss of Emily, I didn't expect our third session to follow quite so closely to our previous one, but then there's nothing like a major life-changer to catapult us into action. After a warm greeting and taking our seats, Frank took some papers out of his briefcase and placed them on the coffee table while Jerome added a sketch pad to the heap. Obviously, they had both completed their assignment from our earlier session. Without saying a word, we glanced down at the table and then up at each other—up down, up down—it seemed to go on ad infinitum as the atmosphere vibrated with expectancy, accompanied by an unspoken acknowledgment that the "expected" hadn't yet arrived. And so it passed that in silent agreement we waited. But not for too long.

"Spirit is telling me you've made a significant decision since the boys moved in," I said, piercing the silence, "and to trust the direction in which your hearts are taking you."

"We took the boys to Belize during spring break," Frank began. "We purposely didn't tell them it was a vacation and kept things as close to how they would be on any ordinary day to see how they would relate to the people and overall environment. I never could have imagined what happened next. While the boys were playing on the beach in front of the restaurant where we were having lunch, Jerome and I couldn't help overhearing a conversation taking place at the next table where two couples were sitting. When one of the men said, 'I'm not sure what we'll do if someone doesn't buy our place,' that was all Jerome needed to hear. The next thing I knew he was standing at the table where the folks were sitting and made a public service announcement that we were interested in buying property in the area."

Jerome takes over from there. "So the man says, 'My wife and I have been running a small, exclusive fishing business for over twenty years and put it on the market two years ago because we want to return to the States to be with our new grandchild before we get any older.'

"I knew Frank had heard the man's description of the property," he continued, "So all that was left to do was set the day and time for a visit, which was the next day. After our tour, when we got in the car, Frank says to me, 'Is your heart telling you the same thing mine is telling me?' "

At that point in their sharing, Frank picks up the sketch pad from the coffee table and hands it to me along with a photo he took on his phone when they visited the property. Behold! There it was—the fishing business, the home, and a charming little storefront right next door. Suddenly, all the earlier perceived obstacles were removed and away the four of them went to Belize. When they came to see me during a visit to the US, they joyfully informed me that whenever they are faced with making a decision the question is no longer

"How?," but rather "What is my heart saying?" And my own heart overflowed with joy when they shared that they have taught Brent and Ryan how to ask themselves the same question and listen for the answer.

From Head to Heart,
Intellect to Intelligence

When you consider the idioms we use to describe the attributes of the heart, things like: "We talked heart-to-heart," "My heart jumped for joy," "I love you from the bottom of my heart," "This comes straight from my heart," "I got to the heart of the matter," "He had a change of heart"—the recommendation to "listen to your head, not your heart" seems counterintuitive.

Maybe you've offered those same words of advice to yourself when faced with making a deeply personal decision. Or when a life choice didn't turn out well, counseled yourself that "Next time I'll be sure to use my head, not my heart." It wouldn't be all that surprising really, because society has conditioned us to believe that the mind should be the master of the heart, that following the lead of the heart guides us down the wrong path. But is the heart truly such an untrustworthy culprit, or is it possible we misunderstand the ways in which our heart directs our lives?

The head prefers to be rational, logical, analytical, and judges the heart as being irrational, illogical, recklessly emotional, and naively vulnerable. This fact certainly eliminates any doubt as to why our mind chatter questions or blocks the heart's energy stream of intelligence-guided intuition, sidetracking us once again from an inherent knowing that knows and knows that it knows.

The Exquisite Partnership of Intelligence and Intuition

Intelligence and intuition accompanied us in our birth suitcase as qualities of consciousness, our essential essence, which some call soul. Rather than being competitors engaged in a power struggle for our attention, intelligence and intuition work together in an exquisite, complementary partnership, each being equally necessary in guiding the existential course of our life's journey.

Research conducted at the HeartMath Institute revealed that "the heart has its own intelligence, separate from the brain, which can be tapped into for answers to some of life's most challenging questions. In essence, it appeared that the heart was affecting intelligence and awareness." And here's more good news! According to HeartMath researchers Rollin McCraty, PhD, Raymond Trevor Bradley, PhD, and Dana Tomasino, BA, "Research in the new discipline of neurocardiology shows that the heart is a sensory organ and a sophisticated center for receiving and processing information. The nervous system within the heart enables it to learn, remember, and make functional decisions independent of the brain's cerebral cortex."[2]

What I have shared about the powers of the heart represents a small fraction of the research conducted. My hope is that it has inspired you to do further research and reading, because it can only add to your commitment to raise the volume on your own heart's intuitive guidance.

Mind Chatter Interrupted

Your heart has been chatting to you throughout your life. The question is, do you listen and make choices based on its intuitive intelligence? In case you tend to bypass or press the mute button on its guidance, there's no need to be discouraged, because it always stands in readiness to be in service to you.

Now, if we're honest, we've all had those days that are unfolding with grace and ease when suddenly someone says or does something we interpret as being personally offensive. Our chest tightens, our breathing becomes more shallow, and we instantly disconnect from the heart. It's now "game on," and away we go, enumerating the ways in which we have been violated, justifying our choice to throw down the gauntlet of retaliation. Not to mention those occasions when, with no provocation from the outside, our mind chatter self-bullies us with its insecure, fear-based conditioning: "I can't speak my truth in the staff meeting or I won't look strong enough to lead a department. I have to be authoritative—that's what'll land the promotion I have my eye on!" Or, "If you expose your real feelings she'll walk all over you. You've got to look strong, like you've got it all together." And let's not overlook how mind chatter attempts to intrude into our spiritual practices: "Ugh! My mind is so all over the place I just want to jump off my meditation cushion and run out of the temple! But then I can't risk the chance of not looking like a good meditator."

Then, twenty minutes later, when we receive the offender's apology, sober up on our self-name-calling, or the meditation leader announces, "It's natural for the mind to be restless, so just keep watching the breath without judgment, with loving

kindness toward yourself," we soften, exhale, release the tension in our chest and stomach. Our mind chatter has been
interrupted by heart chatter, as in "What a relief! It's all normal
and my meditation is going well."

Richard, an army general living in Monterey, California,
was dropped off at my Carmel office by his military driver.
Once we sat down, from the manner in which Richard's body
was fidgeting, coupled with his faltering effort to articulate his
reason for seeing me, I understood that he still felt awkward
seeking out the services of a medium, even in what was by
this time our third session. But that didn't stop spirit from
consistently asking Richard the same parting question at the
end of our session: "Why are you in the military?" to which
Richard responded, "Well . . . why doesn't this spirit of yours
know the military is my life's calling and always has been since
I was a child?" There being no immediate response from spirit
for me to transmit, I simply offered Richard a warm smile and
handshake upon his departure.

During our next visit, spirit changed things up and had
this message for me to deliver as Richard was leaving: "Your
head has been conditioned to believe that you were called to
the military, but it was never the truth of your heart. What is
your heart telling you?"

Imagine my surprise to see this six-foot-four uniformed gentleman whose chest was adorned with pins of all sizes and colors
announcing his honorific achievements break down in tears in
my doorway. "You're right . . . No, I mean spirit is right. I come
from generations of men in the military and never even considered any other option but to carry on the family tradition."

"This is very strange," I responded, which was not in
reference to his admission but rather the next message that

immediately began downloading: "I see you sitting in front of a building surrounded by tall, majestic trees. There's a white house off to the side whose first floor functions as an antiques store. To the left of the store area there is a glassed-in room that looks like a gallery of some sort. Spirit is telling me to say that 'You should be carving.'"

"You must have heard wrong," Richard vehemently retorted, "because the only things I carve are steaks! You have a great reputation, Hans, but this time you just might be a little off course, because I couldn't do anything artistic to save my own life!"

Well, he was amused enough to share spirit's message about the house with his wife, who insisted on accompanying him to his next session.

"I may not be convinced," Richard said by way of introduction, but my wife, Gladys, is. She insisted . . . oh you tell him, Gladys."

"The description of the home that you gave my husband is something I saw in a dream about ten years ago and could never get out of my mind. How could you possibly know about it?" she asked incredulously. "I never mentioned the dream to my husband because I thought it was just a dream and didn't mean anything!"

An aside is required here. It's typical of spirit to transmit to me the instruction for clients to draw, design, or write down the dream of their hearts, whether or not it makes sense to them at the time. Their artistic skill at doing so is not at all important; it's the act of giving their dream a form that begins to make its intangibility become tangible. So naturally, spirit directed me to tell Gladys to draw the house she saw in her dream.

A few weeks later I was in a coffee shop when I got a tap

on the shoulder, turned around, and there stood Gladys! She described how she received a call that her aunt, Jenny, who lived in Vermont and whom she had not seen in forty-three years, was dying, and she and Richard went to visit her. When the taxi pulled in front of the house, Gladys was astounded to see that it was an exact replica of the house she had dreamed about ten years ago and, according to spirit's instruction, she had sketched following our last session.

After their visit to Vermont, Richard and Gladys returned to Monterey and life continued as usual until two months later when Aunt Jenny passed away. As it turned out, the aunt had no living relative other than Gladys, so she and Richard inherited the home along with a sizable amount of cash. Most humbly, in our next session Richard accepted that the next stage of his life was to be lived in Vermont, so he retired from the military and he and Gladys moved there some weeks later.

Out of respect for Aunt Jenny, they decided to keep the home's gallery open until they sold most of the remaining inventory. One day in walks this gentleman carrying two carved wooden ducks—decoys—which he left to be sold on consignment, along with a block of uncarved wood and carving tools.

It was during Gladys's telling of this story that I learned that Richard had a mild case of insomnia. On one particular sleepless night, he went downstairs and upon entering the gallery began a closer examination of the piece of wood and carving tools left by their customer. Several hours later, to his utter astonishment—not to mention Gladys's—he had carved a mallard duck! Soon thereafter the gallery became his studio and he not only found his calling as a master carver, he also won many awards throughout the United States and Canada for his carvings of ducks, geese, and swans.

During our last session, which was by phone, I asked Richard, "What is the most important thing spirit has ever said to you?" To which he unhesitatingly responded, "What is your heart telling you?"

To the sublime simplicity of that singular question, I add: When you trust the intuitive intelligence of the heart, then a possibility becomes a probability, which becomes a reality.

Today's Special: Mind Chatter or Heart Chatter à la Carte

In his book *The Untethered Soul*, Michael Singer writes, "You will come to see that the mind talks all the time because you gave it a job to do."[3] What he's saying, in essence, is that both mind chatter and heart chatter are à la carte selections on our inner menu, and we place our order based upon the dictates of our mental-emotional taste buds.

It's helpful to understand that while you can attempt and even succeed in suppressing or bypassing mind chatter, this doesn't mean it's been eliminated from the menu. What's happened is that it has simply gone underground, into the subconscious, only to resurface once it gets triggered.

Then there's another strategy we employ which is affirming the opposite of a negative thought, feeling, or emotion, which sounds more like the heart is speaking to us. Whether such affirmations are verbal, mental, or posted on our refrigerator, they make us feel as though we are more in control, more secure, or soon will be, because we are endeavoring to convince ourselves that the positivity we have affirmed will become our reality. *Mind chatter, whether negative or positive, is still mind chatter.* Even though high-minded chatter feels better to us and offers some relief, it is no substitute for the heart's intuitive intelligence, which transmits to us the objective, unvarnished truth. That being said, affirmations can succeed in calming us down and for that reason contribute to our being able to open and begin reconnecting to the intelligence of the heart.

What is the ultimate remedy for this unrelenting human predicament? Yelling or pleading with the voice of mind chatter to go away won't help. Distracting oneself with more distractions is pointless. *The main practice is to train in awareness.* This means being aware of when we're beginning to get all caught up and swept away, taking a deep breath, and letting go.

The more we train in being aware, the more we will succeed in connecting with and receiving the heart's intuitive guidance throughout our daily activities. Then, when challenges, opportunities, and perplexities present themselves, we will be prepared to follow the wisdom of our heart.

Bringing It All Home

TRAIN IN AWARENESS

+ Write down a challenge, decision, or question you are currently facing.
+ Regardless of what you previously determined about it or input received from other sources, open yourself to receiving fresh, intuitive guidance.
+ Focus your awareness in the heart center and enter a meditative awareness, remaining there for at least fifteen minutes. As thoughts arise, simply say "thinking," and return to watching your breath.

+ Invite guidance to come through by inwardly asking,
  "What is my heart saying?"
+ Let yourself simply be an objective scribe, recording
  what comes through without judging or editing it.
+ Read what you have written and check in with
  yourself to see if it vibes, then read it again.
+ If your guidance has prescribed specific actions, ask
  for direction on the timing for implementing them.
+ Record the results of your actions so that you may
  witness how they take shape, as this will build your
  trust in your heart's intuitive intelligence.

To enhance and expand your ability to work with mind chatter, visit the link below for free resources:
  www.GuidedBook.com/mindchatter

CHAPTER 10

✳

Nurturing Our Children's Clairsentience and Related Abilities

BY THE TIME of early childhood there is something notice-ably "different" about mediumistic, clairaudient, clairvoyant, psychic, or highly clairsentient children. In fact, without proper support, it is possible for them to experience confu-sion, self-consciousness, self-rejection, and even self-imposed isolation. Fortunately for me, my dear father recognized my mediumistic abilities early on and in his wisdom nurtured both them and me. I attribute this to his qualities of open-mindedness and kindheartedness. When, for example, I would share with him clairsentient knowledge I had about my grand-father and great-grandfather, he was delighted rather than frightened or skeptical. How lovingly he assured me that my gifts were as natural as those of children who could paint, play music, or express other talents considered incongruent with their physical age, earning them the title "prodigy."

Of course not all adults are prepared to encounter children

with highly developed clairsentient and related capacities. For example, there are times when it seems like just yesterday that I was sitting in my grade school classroom gazing out the window at the trees and birds when all at once, on a wave of transporting energy, I would teleport outdoors. At that age, it was an organic experience for which I didn't yet have a name. My teachers did, however, and they made frequent use of it: "Hans! Get out of your imagination and back into this classroom, right now!" Perhaps you, too, have memories of childhood magic that you convinced yourself was only imaginary?

We Are All Beneficiaries of Societal Conditioning

The ego's need for a sense of individual safety and security has led us to accept the illusion of having control over life as long as we live by the societal conditioning extended to us by institutions including family, education, culture, religion, and government. A harmful side effect of this mindset is that in order to avoid upsetting the authority figures in their lives, children don't feel safe sharing that they were visited by an angel, a spirit playmate, or a deceased relative in the spirit world. Sadly, this also prevents them from conveying messages from their visitors that have the potential to bring comfort and healing to the child's family members and others.

In general, because of their physical dependence, children are seen as helpless beings, as vessels into which intelligence and other qualities must be pumped in from the outside. Rare are the parents who are aware that their child's birth suitcase has been packed with everything that is required for living his or her purpose, for accomplishing his or her soul's work. One of the greatest gifts parents can give to themselves and their children is to go beyond the logic and rationality of the mind and listen to the inherent intuition and wisdom of the heart. What holds parents back? The fears, superstitions, insecurities, dogmas, and limitations instilled in them by their own societal conditioning, which they in turn bequeath unto their children.

Out of the need for parental and eventually societal approval, a child begins to live a life that has been created *for it* rather than *by it*, thereby desensitizing the inherent awareness of her uniquely individual life path. The sacred responsibility that has been entrusted to parents is to grow their children *toward* and not away from their authentic self. The good news is that through our innate clairsentience, at any age and stage in life we can retrace our soul's footsteps back to the purpose for which we have incarnated.

Let's take a deeper look into the dynamics of how what has been described thus far plays out through some real-life stories that have unfolded during my sessions with parents and their children.

A Buddhist Monk Named Laurel

Because the benefits of parental support cannot be overemphasized, I wish to share with you an example of what it looks like when, at the very outset, parents trust and act upon their child's clairsentience.

"This is our daughter Laurel," her parents shyly began

during our first session. "She is eight years old and a rein-carnated Buddhist monk." Their claim rang so true I swear I could hear a temple gong singing in agreement!

Taking Laurel gently by the hand, she and I walked across the room and sat together at a table. "Would you like to draw me a picture of who you were in your previous life?" I asked, placing a pad and pen before her. Without hesitating, in what took about four minutes, Laurel drew an Asian-looking leaf with a long-plumed bird perched next to it.

"So," I asked, "where are you in this picture?"

"I'm the bird," she matter-of-factly stated.

"And what are you doing?" I inquired.

With a smile radiating pure and utter contentment she said, "Nothing. I'm just being." Then, in a tone of inner authority far beyond her years she announced, "And I don't want to live here anymore! I want to be in the country I came from!"

Laurel's parents began to self-consciously fidget, their eyes welling up with tears of love mixed with what felt like an inevitable loss of their daughter. In their hearts they longed to do what was best for her yet felt torn about how to respond to Laurel's insistence on moving away from her family home at such a young age. You see, Laurel felt out of place not only with her schoolmates and playmates, with whom she had nothing in common, but equally so with her two sisters. Laurel's parents were looking to me to consult with their daughter's guides so that clarity could be provided for the highest good of all concerned.

I'm so pleased to report that soon after our session Laurel was enrolled in a Buddhist-oriented school that hosts visiting monks from Nepal, Bhutan, and India. Fast forward ten years and she is now an eighteen-year-old living in a Buddhist temple on Kauai, fulfilling her karma and dharma. What an immeasurable blessing for Laurel that her parents related to her not as their "product" to chisel according to their design, but instead respected her as an individual with a life purpose uniquely her own. It is because of their unconditional love and trust that Laurel was able to exert her clairsentient awareness of her dharma and begin fulfilling it so early in her life.

Freddie's Visitation

Elizabeth was twenty-eight years old when her mother's friend recommended that she have a session with me. After exchanging a warm greeting on the morning of our meeting, Elizabeth began taking her seat when all at once a handsome man around her age instantly appeared at her side. Tenderly placing his hand on her right shoulder he implored me, "Please, tell her that I love and miss her so much and am deeply sorry our lives were tragically split apart." In a matter of seconds he transmitted to me that he had died in a motorcycle accident when a drunk driver sped through a stop sign, catapulting him seventy feet into the air. He was killed instantly, right before Elizabeth's eyes. I could only imagine the depth of her shock and grief as she knelt before her deceased husband, seven months pregnant with their child. Two months later, Elizabeth gave birth to a beautiful son for whom she and Michael had chosen the name Freddie.

Before sharing her husband's message from the spirit world, I waited for Elizabeth to tell me the purpose for which she had requested our session. She began by pouring out her heart's pain about how she had lost her beloved husband just two months shy of Freddie's birth. At the appropriate juncture, when I delivered Michael's message, tears of joy commingled with relief poured down Elizabeth's cheeks. She had made peace with Michael's passing, she told me, and had been waiting for signs of Freddie's readiness to learn about his father. In her description of events as they unfolded, I realized what Elizabeth was seeking in our session was quite simple: validation that her interpretation of Freddie's process was as beautiful as it appeared to be, that she could wholeheartedly trust in its authenticity. Here is what she shared amid tender tears.

Freddie was three years old and had just begun to speak in short sentences. One day, he shockingly announced to his mother, "Daddy is here." Needing a moment to absorb the implication of his words, the only response Elizabeth could muster was to furrow her brow and incredulously ask, "What did you say?"

Freddie added directional body language to his statement: "Daddy is right *there*," he said, pointing to a specific location in the room.

Elizabeth interpreted this developmental milestone as an indicator that Freddie was ready to be introduced to his father and to be told how much he had been looking forward to his birth. This is how she relayed their continuing conversation.

"Honey," she began, lifting little Freddie upon her lap, "before you were born, your daddy was in an accident that took him away from us. Now he's in heaven watching over us. He . . ."

"No!" Freddie authoritatively protested. "Daddy is here. *I see Daddy.*"

Now, immediately after the accident, Elizabeth had removed all of the photos of Michael from throughout the house to spare Freddie from feeling the loss of the father he never got to know, so she couldn't fathom how he could possibly have known to call the man he claimed to see "Daddy." From that point on, whenever Freddie said he was seeing his father, Elizabeth lovingly smiled at his insistence, assuming that he wanted to have a daddy like his playmates and that at some point he would surely outgrow the need to create an imaginary daddy.

What followed a little over a year later mystified her even more profoundly. Early one evening when mother and son were playing a game together, Freddie interrupted their fun saying, "Mommy, Daddy says to take the pictures out of the garage and put them in the house."

"What? What pictures are you talking about?" she asked.

"Daddy says it's OK now," Freddie continued. "He wants me to see what he looks like."

Pin-drop silence filled the space between us. Regaining her composure, Elizabeth then rhetorically asked me, "I mean, how could he possibly have been talking about the photos of Michael that he never even knew existed?"

I compassionately nodded as Elizabeth described how she staggered to the garage in what felt to be an altered state, obediently retrieved the photos, and, following Michael's direction, placed them throughout the house. Freddie was thrilled, and from that point on they began to videotape and record him talking to his father in the spirit world. Needless to say, Elizabeth now fully welcomed Michael's visitations.

Over time, Freddie delivered Michael's messages not only to Elizabeth, but also to Michael's mother and brother. Elizabeth was not, however, emotionally prepared for Michael's next instruction. "Daddy wants you to be happy. He doesn't want you to be alone anymore," Freddie advised her. Michael further committed to helping Elizabeth find a suitable life-partner and loving stepfather to Freddie.

To say this announcement radically changed Elizabeth's life would be an understatement. Its soul-stretching effect gave her permission to go beyond her pain, beyond her limited definition of fidelity to her deceased husband and stand in a complete "Yes!" Not long after, Elizabeth met and married a wonderful man who was a devoted stepfather to Freddie and, to his joy, he even gained a baby sister.

Throughout the years Elizabeth and I have had occasional sessions. Not surprisingly, Freddie's teen years brought their unique rites of passage. When he naively shared with friends how his father appears and speaks to him, they teased him good-naturedly. He grew to realize that what was so natural for him could be foreign to his peers, so he began to apply more discernment in his sharing. As of this writing, Freddie is a good student, a happy, well-rounded young man who considers his dad to be his best friend and guardian angel.

Alan and Jason Regenerate Their Bond

Alan, a client bent on molding his seventeen-year-old son according to his parental design, came to me frustrated that he could not persuade Jason to give up his passion to be an actor. In Alan's case, his own father came forth and transmitted to me this message: "I'm so sorry, son, that because I didn't first get to know you, you were prevented from becoming who you were meant to be and instead became who I wanted you to be." Then came these poignant words, "And now I see that you're making the same mistake with your own son."

At this point Alan broke down, but his mental habit pattern still overrode his heart's vulnerability. "I can't let my son be an actor! It's a road filled with heartache," he protested.

Alan's father wasted no time interjecting his opinion, saying, "This attitude isn't coming from *you*. It's coming from what *I imposed on you*."

Unable to digest his father's words, there Alan sat, concretized in his mindset, completely unaware of the truth in his father's vigorous attempt to identify the source of his son's stubbornness.

"So now does he . . . I mean do you . . . well, whoever in the hell it is, am I now expected to go home and tell my son that I support him in becoming an actor?" Alan stammered.

"Yes," I calmly replied, "but it has to be sincere if it's going to have an impact."

"Well, I just can't do it! There are so many things about that industry I don't approve of," he righteously added.

Recognizing that he was in a self-defense mode I responded, "Let me get this straight. Are you saying you're choosing to potentially lose your relationship with your son over compromising on what you are convinced are your personal values?"

"Absolutely," he confirmed, accompanied by vigorous head shaking.

Following a couple more sessions, Alan finally accepted my advice that he see a psychologist and read some books I recommended. As a result, he began to loosen his grip on the preconceived notion that if his son didn't follow in his footsteps and those of his grandfather by becoming an accountant, he would be guilty of familial disloyalty by breaking their professional lineage. Love finally overrode his cherished opinions about what was best for his son's life. The happy result for them both was that his son began to trust his father's encouragement of his aspiration to become an actor and in time their bond as father and son flourished.

Jeremy and Uncle Jack

There are children who come into this lifetime firmly anchored in their sense of purpose and do not become sidetracked by their parents. An example is Jeremy, a client who up until the age of ten received nightly visits from an English gentleman who introduced himself to Jeremy saying, "Call me Uncle Jack."

Uncle Jack taught Jeremy about the life force sustaining the cosmos, shimmering in the sky and stars, flowing in tree trunks, the roots of all plants, and how to perceive their spirits. He also taught him some esoteric healing arts. Innocently assuming that everyone had such visitations from the spirit world, Jeremy told his parents about Uncle Jack and the things he learned from him. Although they endured Jeremy's sharing for a while, when they felt it was time for him to outgrow these "imaginary conversations" with his "imaginary friend," they sent him to a therapist.

"You know, Uncle Jack is not real. He's a figment of your imagination lodged in your subconscious that comes out to play from time to time," the therapist pontificated with biblical authority.

"No," Jeremy protested, "you're wrong! I *know* Uncle Jack. I've always known him."

It took two years before Jeremy's parents and therapist managed to wear him down to the point where he stopped talking openly to and about Uncle Jack. By the time of our next session, Jeremy was a young man. Wouldn't you know that the first person who came to me with a message for Jeremy was—*you guessed it*—Uncle Jack! Jeremy's clairsentience had clairvoyant overtones, so he was able to effortlessly reconnect with Uncle Jack. His life changed immeasurably, restoring his passion for his purpose on the planet.

One day when Jeremy returned some books I had loaned him, he joyfully announced, "All my life I've wanted to make a difference in the world by serving others through the healing arts, and now I'm on my way to doing that, thanks to Uncle Jack."

No Child Is a Blank Page

Early childhood is a pivotal time when children are either permitted to or prevented from following their clairsentient knowledge of their karma and dharma. Parents, conditioned to consider their child to be a blank page, assume they know what to write on that page about what he or she must become. This should come as no surprise, since as a society we act as though intelligence, creativity, wisdom, joy, and other qualities must be pumped in from the outside. We don't credit our Creator Source with already having equipped us with all that we require to live our life purpose.

It bears repeating: No child is a blank page. Each and every spirit-soul arrives on the planet with a custom-designed letter-head that includes a mission statement. Not realizing this, parents rewrite it, convinced about what should appear as its header—my daughter's purpose is to be a ballerina, just like her Russian grandmother; my son will be the next president of our winery—and they go about indoctrinating their children with these notions.

It was long, long ago when spirit gave me this message: *Parents grow their children out of who they are, and thereby, out of their potential to be who they are meant to be.* When required, I gently share that message with parents and more frequently than not they get teary eyed. A deep-rooted soul-memory res-urrects itself, reminding them that this happened to them as children and they have now bequeathed this misguided legacy unto their children. And it's now time to stop.

Bringing It All Home

When a child bares his soul, it is important for parents not to brush it off, to disregard what he is saying simply because he is very young. If a parent attempts to dissuade him from what he intuitively knows, his connection to his guidance may begin to erode. And because spirit guides do not impose upon anyone, they also pull back. Neither of these conditions is desirable.

There are two time-tested antidotes I recommend for pre-venting parental intrusion into a child's inherent soul-wisdom. First, when your child is about three years old, purchase a video camera and a recorder and keep them near at hand. Now this isn't for sentimental recordings of your children's growth history or first tricycle ride; it is for the purpose of capturing directly from them how, as parents, you can profoundly contribute to nurturing their intuitive and related capacities. Second, ask and record their responses to these five questions:

+ Who are you?
+ What have you come on the planet to learn in this lifetime?
+ What have you come on the planet to do in this lifetime?
+ What can we do to help you?
+ Is there anything else you want us to know about you?

On the surface, these questions may appear to be overly sophisticated and in language beyond a child's vocabulary. Don't be fooled! The energy of respect and unconditional love expressed through these questions is received and understood by a child's spirit-soul. Granted, this process will no doubt require more than one "take" at the various ages and stages of a child's development, but the results I have personally witnessed and those that have been shared with me by parents are enough to stop questioning a child's inherent soul-knowledge. When parents remain open, nonthreatened, nonjudgmental, and encourage a child's ongoing revelations, tremendous evolutionary progress is made; parents are fulfilling their purpose for being parents, and the child is lovingly led into living his authentic life path. I also encourage parents to relax in the understanding that simply because a child has activated her innate quality of intuition, it does not mean that her life purpose is to become a professional reader.

SUPPORTING YOUR CHILD'S
CLAIRSENTIENT AND RELATED ABILITIES

The guidance I offer parents who suspect their children have activated their clairsentient and related abilities is to make it their topmost priority to educate themselves on these abilities. As you will have observed from the stories shared in this chapter, rather than the child fearing his or her gifts, it is the parents who, in most cases, are afraid. I wish also to acknowledge that when a child describes otherworldly events that the parents have not themselves experienced, it is natural for their immediate response to be one of concern, denial, or fear, which may in turn cause them to seek out therapists or related professionals. (Fortunately, we can all give a sigh of grateful relief that today's society and science now share a more evolved acceptance of what is possible in consciousness.)

Parental education contributes greatly to eliminating any fear that a child is afflicted in a negative manner, that in fact such gifts have tremendous spiritual content and value. For example, consider how every scripture of the world's religions has recorded instances of individuals—everyday people—who have used their innate intuitive abilities for counseling, guiding, healing, and comforting others.

Most importantly, once a child's ability begins to emerge, it may continue to expand, or other related abilities may begin to reveal themselves. Your child will need to be able to rely on you as a parent to relate to her, to let her know you understand and support her ability, and to share in her gifts. She deeply desires that you pay attention to what she shares with you, that you take her seriously and do not fear, deny, or denigrate her. As well, it is vital to honor her privacy and not speak of her gifts in front of her with others or, for that matter, even privately, unless you have prior knowledge that a person will be open and honor your sharing with confidentiality. If you feel the need to speak about your child and her abilities, seek out recommendations for a professional reader with trustworthy credentials. As my clients have demonstrated, tremendous comfort comes from speaking with a time-tested and proven reader.

IDENTIFYING YOUR CHILD'S INTUITIVE AND RELATED ABILITIES

If your child shares with you one or more of the following experiences, it is likely that he/she has activated the quality of clairsentience and/or related abilities:

+ Your child describes a person who appears to him and shares with him guidance about his life.
+ Your child expresses a curiosity about a deceased family member whom she has never met in person, or says that such a person has visited her.
+ Your child says he has been to a country or place even though he hasn't.
+ Your child exhibits an urge to place her hands on people or animals to help them feel better.
+ Your child describes another time in history, a person, place, or a spiritual practice in such graphic detail that it appears to have been a part of her soul's experience.
+ Your child uses vocabulary or makes specific references to knowledge that indicates insightfulness beyond his years.

✦ Your child shares with you other lifetimes he has
  lived on the Earth plane or realms beyond the third
  dimension.
✦ Your child asks about the reality of angels or spirits,
  more than likely sparked by having had such
  encounters and is now "checking in" about your
  response before sharing the facts with you.
✦ Your child expresses feeling "different" or ostracized
  by classmates and/or playmates, or bullied by them
  due to having shared one of his clairsentient or
  clairvoyant experiences.
✦ Your child asks why other children don't hear or see
  things that she does.

Certainly there are more criteria for identifying your child's
clairsentient and related abilities. My intention here is to provide just some of the examples you may use as an incentive that
will set you in the direction of educating yourself more fully,
and especially for offering the nurturance required by your
highly sensitive, empathic, and clairsentient child.

CHAPTER 11

✳

Learning to Laugh
Like a Buddha

THERE WAS A time when wearable technology for measuring how many steps we take in a day, how many calories we burn, monitoring our heart rate while walking, cycling, and hiking bordered on science fiction. Undoubtedly, in a time not too far away, technology-equipped textiles will be worn by models walking Paris runways. And perhaps even land in our own closets and sock drawers! My question is, wouldn't it be a great addition if someone invented a wearable monitor to measure the surge of endorphins that are released every time we laugh? Nanotechnology visionaries appear to be overlooking a great opportunity here! I wonder if any of them are aware of Dr. William F. Fry's research at Stanford University, which proved that "Laughter stimulates the production of the alertness hormones, catecholamine," which in turn "cause the release of endorphins in the brain."[1]

As the Bible tells us in Proverbs 17:22, "A merry heart does good, like medicine, but a broken spirit dries the bones." Indeed, laughter is known to raise good cholesterol and lower inflammation in the heart as well as providing "the diaphragm, thorax, abdomen, heart, lungs, and even the liver a massage during a hearty laugh," says Dr. Marvin E. Herring, a family practitioner at New Jersey School of Osteopathic Medicine. Doesn't that make you want to laugh just for the health of it? There's a late 1980s *New York Times* article I never forgot which described how nurses at an Oregon hospital wore buttons that said "Warning: Humor May Be Hazardous to Your Illness." How true, for each of us is one organic whole, a total unity of being, so it comes down to everyday wisdom that laughter benefits us in body, mind, and spirit.

Sometimes just watching others laugh without even knowing why they're laughing causes a chain of contagion to spread among those who witness it; they simply can't resist laughing along, even when they're not in on the joke. It's irresistible, and more infectious than a cough or a cold.

In the November 2000 issue of *Psychology Today*, Robert R. Provine, a neurobiologist and professor of psychology who studies laughter, published an article titled "The Science of Laughter" in which he writes, "Stripped of its variation and nuance, laughter is a regular series of short vowel-like syllables usually transcribed as 'ha-ha,' 'ho-ho,' or 'hee-hee.' These syllables are part of the universal human vocabulary, produced and recognized by people of all cultures. Given the universality of the sound, our ignorance about the purpose and meaning is remarkable."[2] His last sentence really struck me, and when viewed through his lens, laughter is a rather serious matter!

A Healthy Ego Includes a
Healthy Sense of Humor

Unless one's life-juices have completely dried up, it is impossible not to sense the cosmic smile our Creator Source has spread across all existence and encrypted within the human spirit. My hope is that what I have shared thus far is supporting you in beginning to lighten up on yourself. You can afford to, really, because the journey is largely about *unlearning* what you've been taught and releasing the false perceptions you have embodied. A most effective way to begin loosening the octopus grip of old conditioning pulsing in your marrow is hearty laughter, because when we laugh the body, mind, heart, and spirit all join in.

Of course when it comes to laughing at ourselves—let alone accepting others' laughter at us—ego is blatantly resistant. We forget that anything that crosses swords with our entitled ego is a source of transformation, so we spend far too much time attempting to live up to society's mandate, "Don't make a laughingstock out of yourself." What a humor-challenged edict, especially when considering it would take only a whiz-bang minute to compile a list of individuals who were the laughingstock of their era, only later to be recognized as creative geniuses and spiritual savants!

Ego is the gatekeeper of our image, and its job description includes comparing ourselves to and competing with others in the arena called "success," most often resulting in feelings of inferiority or superiority, neither of which serve as accurate measures of the truth. We compare this week's accomplishments against last week's, and if we haven't met our set goals according to the latest book on what constitutes success, we certainly don't deserve to uncork that celebratory bottle of champagne! Our games of one-upmanship with ourselves hold us hostage, sabotaging our joie de vivre, our cheerful enjoyment of life. Catching ourselves at playing such games liberates us, makes us less serious about seriousness, because we are breaking through the hard shell of the unhealthy ego's expectations along with its projections about what we should be adding to our credential collection and résumé of achievements.

One of the most powerful ways to grow a healthy ego is by having a sense of humor about your quirks, crazies, or whatever name you have for them, which I hope is an affectionate one. Try saying this to yourself the next time you are in the stranglehold of your inner critic's diatribe: "Oh, I see that you, ego, have dropped in for tea masquerading as my conscience. Welcome! Now let's shake hands and share a good laugh about this foolishness." Such nonresistant acknowledgment allows you to let what is occurring in your mind to move on, like a cloud passing in the sky, without your getting swept away by the overthinking, discursive mind.

I cannot recall any session with a client when spontaneous outbreaks of laughter did not open a space for releasing tensions, anxieties, self-sabotaging evaluations, and emotions. Laughter lightens your entire being, allowing you to be receptive to intuitive guidance. When you can genuinely laugh at yourself, you will move more freely and joyously in the world. And you will become more skillful at unpacking your birth suitcase and working with your mystical mirror.

The Zen of Laughter

Legend has it that the Laughing Buddha we see depicted in various statues with a large belly and jocular smile is based on the life of Hotei, an eccentric Buddhist monk who lived in tenth-century China. His jovial countenance, loving heart, and teaching were one: laugh. It's said that as he stood in the middle of a town through which he was passing he would simply laugh and its contagion caused everyone around him to be spontaneously taken over by uncensored, uncontrollable laughter.

On those occasions when a client shares with me that he or she is experiencing laughter deprivation, if I feel guided to do so, I suggest buying a statue of the Laughing Buddha and letting its infectious smile light up their hearts and let a good "ha-ha" turn into an "ah-ha" moment, softening the sharp edges of annoying, negative mind chatter. I often think about how despite the tragedy of having seen so many of his monks and countrymen die while fleeing from Tibet in the late 1950s, and then being forced to live in exile with his people in Dharamsala, India, when you see His Holiness the Dalai Lama interviewed or speaking, the smile of a Buddha lights his face, radiating the contagion of this precious commodity to millions.

In Zen and other Buddhist monasteries, laughter is considered to be a potent daily meditation. Lee Berk, associate professor of pathology and human anatomy at Loma Linda University, discovered this in his laughter research: "Joyful laughter immediately produces the same brain wave frequencies experienced by people in a true meditative state. . . .

Gamma is the only frequency that affects every part of the brain. So when you're laughing, you're essentially engaging your entire brain at once. This state of your entire brain being 'in synch' is associated with contentment, being able to think more clearly, and improved focus."[3]

When we laugh we are wholly in the present moment. We can't laugh and hold a thought at the same time—even when whatever it was that initially set off our laughter disappears. I call this a "laughgasm," because just as in sexual orgasm, we lose our sense of self—all thought disappears and we are at one with the energy of laughter, we are utterly overtaken by it. Thoughts, opinions, hurts, disappointments, credentials, name, fame, to-do lists—all of it . . . gone! We are liberated from the burden of self and enter the state of "no-mind," as it's called in Zen. And a side effect of "no-mind" is "no mind chatter."

Let Laughter Be Your Mantra

Have you ever had the experience of sitting at a restaurant table waiting for a friend to arrive when suddenly, upon detecting the sound of her laughter, you know she is approaching? I doubt that we consciously attempt to remember a person's laugh, and yet it's as though we have a laugh detector that records it in our memory. Suddenly, it registers that the sound of laughter you hear soaring above all the other noise in the restaurant is your friend's, because laughter is as individualized as is the sound of a person's voice.

Our laughter is like a mantra—a verbal sound capable of clearing the mind and creating a transformation that deepens with each repetition. Laughter is a reflection of our inner rhythm emoting through sound, transmitting a vibrational energy that impacts those who hear it and pick up its "vibe."

"I would not exchange the laughter of my heart for the fortunes of the multitudes," wrote Kahlil Gibran in *Tears and Laughter*.[4] What a perfect reminder for us to not be economical with our laughter. How often do you laugh straight from the heart? Or laugh so deeply that your laughter turns into tears of liberation? And how about when engaging in heart-opening laughter at yourself and the antics of your mind chatter? As the wise Swami Beyondananda (aka Steve Bhaerman) writes in "Swami's Daily Laughsitive," "Life is a situation comedy that will never be canceled." So, "whenever irregular hilarity strikes,"[5] all we have to do is look right at our own life and we can always find something to laugh about and enlighten-up our heart and spirit.

The Humorous Adventures of Spirit Guides

When Beverly came to see me, it was to sort out a conundrum that had an octopus grip on her mind and heart for some years after her mother, Angela, had passed away. While Beverly felt her mother did not like her as a person and that they had what she assessed to be a contentious relationship, this conflicted with the fact that her mother had a terrific sense of humor.

"How could a person with such a cheerful nature not have liked me?" was the question constantly reverberating in Beverly's mind and which she now rhetorically placed before me.

Upon contacting her mother in the spirit world, I shared

with Beverly that her mother not only liked her but in fact loved her very much.

"No! If she had of, she would have been much nicer to me," Beverly vehemently retorted, obviously unconvinced.

Then, in what must have been typical of her brand of humor, Angela told me to tell Beverly to "Be on the lookout for the red heels!" When I conveyed this message to Beverly, her facial expression turned to stone and silence filled the space between us.

Just as I'd begun to wonder if I'd stepped into a *Wizard of Oz II* "The Red Shoe Sequel," Beverly's brow furrowed and, dispensing with me, she directed these accusatory words to her mother's spirit, "Why are you teasing me?" End of conversation . . . and the session.

Upon arriving home, Beverly decided to distract herself from thoughts about her mother by doing some laundry, in the middle of which she called me to schedule an immediate second session. Here's how the "Red Shoe Sequel" unfolded.

For Beverly's high school graduation, her mother had given her a present of red patent leather high heels—her very first. She treasured those heels and wore them on every possible occasion. However, she never let her mother see her wearing them out of what you might call an "I'll show you" teenage retaliation against having felt unliked by her mother. Then, once patent leather was no longer in style, Beverly stored the shoes away, and even before the time of our first session she no longer remembered where.

Meanwhile, back at the scene of doing her laundry, when the wash cycle ended, Beverly opened the door to the dryer and behold: *the red patent leather shoes!* Even she couldn't miss the heavenly humor in this incident, evidenced by her guffaws when relating its details to me. That the shoes managed to teleport themselves from their unknown hiding place into the clothes dryer could only have been choreographed by her mother. This, Beverly explained, was indeed a perfect example of the humorous tricks Angela performed when she was alive. Beverly laughed herself into open-hearted tears, and into a healed relationship with her mother. To this day, when she needs a laugh, she herself puts her beloved red patent leather heels in the dryer and shares a good laugh with Angela in the spirit world.

In a spirit of self-disclosure, my own guides generously share with me their sense of humor and laughter, sometimes on a daily basis! They're especially fond of good-naturedly poking fun at my mind chatter, their technique for teaching me to laugh at my mental gymnastics. On one occasion when I was mind chattering away about something that didn't go my way, spirit entered the fray. "Are you going to watch the show?" my master guide inquired. Before I could ask "What show?" he began calling in other members of my guide tribe—"Hey everybody, Hansie is doing his show again!" Having no idea about what "show" I was starring in, I was now more confused than ever, not to mention slightly irritated. So when one of them says to me, "You make our day when you run your crazies," my ego tried to convince me that surely I was misinterpreting that I was the cause of their uproarious laughter. They've done this with me for years! You'd think that I'd have caught on by now, but the nature of mind chatter blinds us to our all-caught-up-ness.

How my guides best succeed in shaking me out of my stupor of mind chatter is when they inform me, "You don't listen to anything you teach!" They know this makes me crabby, but this is also how they play with me to usher me back into the clarity of self-awareness. Believe me—it works! How well our guides know that humor and its resulting laughter at ourselves softens the way we learn our lessons. As the sage Mark Twain once said, "Against the assault of laughter, nothing can stand."

Bringing It All Home

By making your own laughter your mantra and repeating it often, you will be lifted into your higher self and reclaim your childlike quality of wonderment. In addition to practicing the laughing meditation described below, I encourage you to record your laughter. You can do this by watching a funny film segment or watching your children or pets at play—whatever you think will help induce laughter. Then, when you play back the recording, listen deeply and you will feel the waves of its energetic frequency wash over you, enchanting your heart and uplifting your spirit. Just one utterance of your laughing mantra and you will connect to your inner rhythm of joy, which cannot help but keep you laughing.

LAUGHING MEDITATION EXERCISE

You may practice this form of laughing meditation by itself or, if meditation is part of your daily practice, immediately after your meditation session and before you begin your day. And of course you can pause at any time throughout your day to practice it.

+ Place yourself in a comfortable sitting position with your back straight and eyes closed.

+ Slightly part your lips and let your tongue and jaw relax. Then gently rotate your neck in one direction for three turns and then in the opposition for three turns.
+ Open your mouth wide enough to create a yawn or two to further relax the facial muscles.
+ Begin to gently smile, hold for a few seconds and relax. Repeat this three times.
+ Next, begin to laugh out loud. Stop when it feels natural to do so and then laugh again. Notice how your laughter begins to bubble up by itself.
+ When you feel ready, stop laughing and simply rest in the energy.
+ Take the energy of this laughter into your day. When stress arises, mentally tap into the energy waves of laughter just below the surface of your mind.

FOR YOUR LAUGHING
PLEASURE EXERCISE

When you notice your mind chatter driving you crazy, you will benefit from this exercise taught to me by my guides, which in itself causes me to begin laughing halfway through my practice! Their method for being the listener to and the observer of mind chatter's contents creates an objectivity that allows you to see through the web it attempts to weave in your mind, causing you to laugh at yourself with great relief and release!

+ Imagine yourself sitting in an elegantly appointed theater with flawless acoustics. There you are in your

cushy box seat, enthusiastic for the show to begin.
At last—curtain call, and out struts the haughty star:
Mind Chatter, beginning its performance in the
spoken word genre that is so popular today. (You can
even create a comical physical form for your mind
chatter.)

+ As your mind chatter begins to speak its lines, which
are quite familiar to you, you roar, guffaw yourself
into tears of realization that you don't have to accept
its unhealthy messages and the accompanying stress it
causes with its fabrications.

+ At the end of the performance, Mind Chatter
unexpectedly takes ownership of its own
ridiculousness, even sharing with you that its lies can't
actually touch you, *unless you yourself grab ahold of
them*, that they are vapors that only condense into
form if you formulate them into your reality.

+ Showing your appreciation for its self-disclosure of
how it disguises itself as truth, you applaud mind
chatter's fictional performance, and delete its program
from your mental inner net.

+ When it sneakily hacks into your mind and
re-downloads itself, you're now much wiser to its
antics and can simply "unsubscribe" to its newsletter.

Love's Superpowers

IN HIS POEM "The Alchemy of Love," we find the Sufi mystic Rumi ecstatically communing with the Cosmic Beloved as the igniter of the flame of Love:

> *You are the master alchemist.*
> *You light the fire of love*[1]

Kabir, Hafiz, Saint John of the Cross, Saint Teresa of Ávila, Hildegard von Bingen, Tagore, Gibran—these mystical lovers across spiritual traditions transcend their respective paths, which is why we hear them using the same love-intoxicated language to share their most intimate, ecstatic revelations through their poetry and writings.

It may not yet be obvious to you, but this Divine Love is the poetry within your own heart, within your aspiration to evolve your highest potential, the magnet that attracts loved ones to you and you to them, the inducement to perform acts of compassion you never imagined possible, and the common denominator you share with all Existence. For just as a single wave contains all the elements of the ocean, as individual waves that have emerged from the vast ocean of our Creator Source, each of us contains its elements, one of which is unconditional Divine Love.

We human beings possess a superpower of love so accessible, in fact, that sacrificing our own life or donating a body part to save a loved one is not unusual. Not to mention someone donating an organ or giving his/her life to protect or save the life of a perfect stranger. We don't have to look far for examples that unquestionably demonstrate love's superpowers. When religious, racial, political, sexual orientation, or gender bigotry rears its monstrous head, we can turn to servants of humankind—such as Dr. Martin Luther King Jr., Cesar Chavez, Mohandas K. Gandhi, His Holiness the Dalai Lama, Nelson Mandela, Rigoberta Menchú, Malala Yousafzai, Thich Nhat Hanh—to confirm that love is always the ultimate answer. Now, their mothers weren't virgins; they weren't born wearing heroes' capes. It is how they engaged love's superpower of compassionate justice to change hearts for which we love and honor them.

The Eternal Romance

The flame of our Creator Source aglow within us as a unique, individualized expression of itself is what we call soul, and is made from the imperishable tissue of spirit. It is the indestructible spark of Divine Love interpenetrating all sentient beings and cosmic creation.

In his interpretation of the *Bhagavad Gita*, Paramahansa Yogananda describes the soul in this way: "It is unborn, though born in a body; it is eternal, though its bodily dwelling is impermanent; it is changeless, though it may experience change; it is ever the same, though in the long pathway of reincarnation which ultimately leads to God, the soul appears in countless forms; the soul is not slain when the body dies; and even when the soul returns to spirit, it does not lose its identity, but will exist unto everlastingness."[2]

The mystics of the world's wisdom traditions refer to spirit as the one Eternal Beloved of the individual soul, which of all mystical experiences is of the utmost rapture, yet not necessarily the soul's ultimate expression while encased in a human form. Fulfilling our dharma and karma and thereby freeing ourselves from the wheel of birth and death in the three-dimensional realm is the ultimate consummation of our life's purpose. Even when we evolve to the point where we inhabit the fourth-dimensional realm, we do our work there in preparation for inhabiting an even higher realm, for as Jesus points out, "In my father's house there are many mansions." We are beneficiaries of spirit's vast celestial real estate, and as we evolve within each dimension we move closer to its neighborhood that defies description.

It may be comforting to know that our human mind does not need to recall all of our incarnations in the earthly and astral dimensions in order to evolve, although an appropriate time will arrive when each of us will come face-to-face with them. The main point is that *your spirit-soul does remember*, and your doorkeeper and master guide have sufficient knowledge of those lifetimes, which are relevant to their work with you. Remember, you are their assignment, which means their own continuing evolution depends on their work in supporting you with your own.

Rising in Love

When it comes to expanding our understanding of the nature of love, for the most part our endeavors are concentrated outwardly, such as reading books and attending seminars on how to attract a love relationship or how to improve or heal a love relationship be it with our partner, children, parents, a sibling, or friend. And while all concerned can thankfully benefit from these valuable resources, it is when we take up interior practices that connect us directly to love's source at the core of our being that we begin to mature our capacity to love unconditionally, to reach a depth of compassion and forgiveness that heals and transforms.

Divine Love changes the entire climate of our inner being. At times we may be satisfied with our efforts—like when writing a heartfelt love letter, when tenderly whispering words of love into the ear of our child, expressing affection to a friend, lovingly caring for an ailing parent, wholeheartedly being there for a sibling's life challenge, rescuing a shelter animal, volunteering in a cause that touches our hearts. What we discover is that we are all love-masters in training, that our human love relationships continuously offer us opportunities to grow our love-capacity. And as we do, no longer do we fall in love—we *rise* in love. We are transfigured, because Divine Love is an alchemical energy that transmutes the base metal of ego into the pure gold of the heart.

Love and Relationship in the Spirit World

At this point you are quite likely asking what all this has to do with relationships with loved ones in the spirit world. Fair enough! There is literally a conga line of dear ones from your more recent incarnations and those of lifetimes ago who are inhabiting various levels of the spirit world. At different stages and in different aspects of your life, a number of them are assigned to serve as your guides. Some are those with whom you have made agreements while together, and with others no formal agreement was made. Perhaps the relationship ended on a sour note and it is only now that both of you are ready to make amends or complete unfinished business. If such relationships enter your awareness out of seeming nowhere, it's quite likely whomsoever is involved is reaching out to you from the spirit world. It would be the higher part of wisdom not to pass up such an opportunity and instead to check it out through a session with a medium or directly with a guide with whom you are currently communicating.

Now, while the human mind would like to organize past and present relationships and their karmic details in a predictable, controllable, and tidy fashion, it is good that it is not possible to do so, for this would not serve their higher purpose. There are subtle realities that the human mind simply cannot wrap itself around, that no spiritual path, regardless of how advanced, can put into human language.

Ultimately, reality itself is ineffable, unfathomable to the human mind. An indicator of spiritual maturity is the ability to peacefully co-exist with this paradox. That being said, what most of us tend to do is work with the everyday realities that comprise our lives. We concentrate on the incarnation we're currently inhabiting and the relationships that are a part of it, including our loved ones who have transitioned to the spirit world. We miss them and want the comfort of knowing that they are happy and adjusted to their new dimension of living.

It is the vibrational density of the earthly realm which causes us to forget that they have returned to a sphere in which they have lived countless numbers of lifetimes, one in which they are having the exquisite experience that accompanies freedom from the ills of the human body and chattering mind. And because we forget, we reach out for confirmation that all is well with them. It is equally helpful to understand that those on the other side are quite busy! Far from strumming harps all day, they are working with their guides, teachers, and astral families in fulfilling their astral dharma and karma.

Individual souls who no longer require returning to the earthly realm reincarnate in one of the various astral spheres where they are born into an astral family based on their evolutionary progress. There they come into contact with friends and relatives from many, many lifetimes. This is not to say that by no longer requiring human birth they have forgotten us, for the more evolved the spirit-soul the clearer is their intuitive soul-memory of all of their previous incarnations and the loved ones with whom they shared them. They may at times be assigned to us as our guides, or as a guide to our guides. However, in the here and now, those with whom we have more recently shared a lifetime on the astral or earthly plane are more frequently involved in interacting with us as we are with them.

I pray that this chapter's contents have served you where both the Divine and human aspects of love are concerned. Taking a deeper view into the fires of initiation through which we pass on our journey to Divine Love fuels our spirit-soul with inspiration, courage, and trust, a journey that will culminate in an explosion of love-energy we cannot humanly comprehend. Just imagine yourself, if you will, standing at the center of the aurora borealis with its rippling curtains and shooting rays of light filling every direction—above, beneath, within, and all around you. That is what the mystical lovers offer us—a glimpse into a love so ecstatic, so penetrating, so transporting that we cannot help surrender to its all-consuming force. And while no words in any human language can adequately describe such an experience, such lovers are compelled to do so, perhaps to impel us to begin our own pilgrimage home to Divine Love.

The words that close this chapter represent my heart's deepest desire and effort to convey that upon awakening your full love-capacity, it will be accompanied by the realization that *all beings are your lovers, friends, children, siblings, mothers, fathers, teachers*. No longer will you be able to limit your love to one or a few individuals. The entire world will be your home and all beings your very own. You will merge in an ecstasy of oneness with every atom of cosmic creation. This is the destination that Divine Love has waiting for you. Not intellectually. Not as a spiritually romantic concept. But as a conscious realization of spirit's cosmic love in and as *you*.

Bringing It All Home

The truth is, it is our Creator Source alone that is our ultimate soul mate. From lifetime to lifetime, spirit is the siren call of

love that we respond to through all of our human relationships. Divine Love is the godliness pulsating within us, but we
have forgotten. Our illusion is that when a love relationship
has completed its purpose in our lives and is over, we mistak-
enly think we have "lost" love. *To lose love itself is impossible.*
Our loved ones are precious vehicles that cause us to expand
beyond the narrow boundaries of "me, myself, and I." They
create in our hearts a passageway through which Divine Love
begins to freely flow and bless all with whom we come in contact. Divine Love never abandons us. It cannot, for it is the
very essence out of which we have been created that breathes
through our breath, beats in our hearts, walks through our
feet, loves through our hearts, that travels within us in every
lifetime, in all realms which we inhabit.

The practice given below is intended to reveal to you the
ever-existing superpower of Divine Love that enlivens your
being, a love so unconditional that it is independent of receiving a response from any person to which you direct it. It is
love as a verb, an action that is always operational within you
once you open the petals of your heart and let it fully bloom.

+ Locate yourself in a private spot where you will not
  be disturbed for about twenty minutes.
+ Taking a meditative posture, close your eyes and
  center your awareness in the heart chakra. Gently
  place your hand over your heart. Inform yourself that
  you are entering Divine Love's sacred chamber within
  you where you will taste its nectar within every atom
  of your being.
+ Without forcing anything, simply breathe. Relax
  into yourself and revel in the sweet contentment

that arises. Soak it in, knowing that you have
come in contact with your Self. Remain there for a
comfortable length of time.

+ When you feel ready, gently move your awareness
back into your body and allow Divine Love to have
its way with you. Let its energy express through
your body whether it's in the form of jumping for
joy, singing whether or not you can carry a tune,
interpreting the energy in dance, or by laughing out
loud, just for the pure joy of it.

+ With the innocence of a child, you have now risen in
love.

To enhance and expand your understanding of soul mate relationships, visit the link below for free resources:
www.GuidedBook.com/soulmates

✳

You Are Your Own Religion

YOUR LIFE IS itself your one true religion. While spiritual teachers, guides, and practices profoundly contribute to accelerating one's inner evolutionary progress, *it is only in the laboratory of your own life that you can consummate the practices that awaken you to the sublime reality of your being.* And as you do, you will bow in awe before the majesty of the life that spirit has entrusted to you. You will realize you were seeking wholeness outside of yourself only because you didn't recognize the wholeness that was already within you. From that point on, no moment will be more spiritually valuable than the one you are in. As Eckhart Tolle poignantly tells us, "The only place where you can find yourself is in the Now."[1] Each now-moment offers itself to you as a mystical mirror of insight, as rich material for internalizing that you already are that which you seek. And for that reason, every moment is potentially momentous.

The human mind can never wrap itself around the ultimate mystery of existence. But what we can be sure of is that each of us has emerged as an individualized wave from the vast ocean of cosmic love that is our origin. Our only problem is that our vision is blurred to the truth, which is, always has been, and always shall be right in front of us. What we seek through all of our seeking is an awakening of our soul-memory of the One out of which came oneself. As Saint Francis of Assisi put it, "What we are looking for is what is looking."

Relationship is a noun, and when it comes to your relationship with yourself, it is surely something to be treasured and enjoyed by everyday standards. Or, it can step up to being a verb, an ever-evolving *relating* to yourself, to your dharma, to courageously stepping out of the status quo, to taking a deeper seat within yourself and becoming more conscious of consciousness, your essential essence.

When it comes to assessing where you stand as far as completing your cycle of incarnating in the third dimension, surrender that effort! It may be that you came on the planet to work out just one remaining karmic imperative, causing it to stand out all the more. You can't hide it from yourself or, perhaps even more frustratingly, from anyone else. You judge yourself and feel judged by others about this overarching nemesis of a specific trait or habitual pattern of behavior. Relax! You're truly much closer to being victorious than you can imagine.

At the end of each chapter, you have been invited to participate in a Bringing It All Home practice. I have no doubt that you have identified that home address to be your very own spirit-soul. Never stop welcoming yourself home. Relax into the unconditional love that can be found nowhere else but *there*, in that shrine of shrines where spirit cherishes you, caresses you, where the experience described in these words of the Sufi mystic, Hafiz, will come alive to you:

And, for no reason,
I start skipping like a child.[2]

The yearning that motivates our inner search also energizes our willingness to begin the spiritual warrior's courageous journey into the core of our being where, as physicist Brian Swimme wrote with such poetic wisdom in *The Universe Is a Green Dragon,* "The universe shivers with wonder in the depths of the human."[3] This is the truth of your own heart, where it beats in rhythm with the Cosmic Heart in a perfection of love that has no comparison.

And so dear friends, my prayer is that through this book I have succeeded in holding before you the mystical mirror as I described in chapter 2. May it reflect your breathtaking beauty exactly as "universe shivers in wonder" at the depths of you.

It has been such a joy to share with you what has been revealed to me on my personal journey, as well as that which I have learned *from you,* my companions whose presences have hovered around me throughout the writing of every chapter. My wholehearted wish is that your mind chatter has become muted and that your trust in your inherent intuitive voice, your clairsentience, has deepened. Know that by leaning into your heart's intuitive intelligence more and more, it will continue to enhance all aspects of your life and the lives of those who surround you.

We are a culture that is increasingly driven by technology, and in some instances spiritual practices are beginning to be considered technologies that work like Windows 7, where just the touch of a button and abracadabra, results are instantaneous. I say this so that you may avoid the trap of becoming impatient with yourself, so that you work within the laboratory of your consciousness with humility, patience, compassion, and loving kindness toward yourself.

When you find yourself standing in the face of a challenge welcome it, knowing that it holds before you a self-reflective mirror revealing the next evolutionary step on your dharmic walk. Trust. Then trust some more. This is how you will wipe the dust from your mystical mirror and come face-to-face with your pristine Self.

Acknowledgments

I WISH TO acknowledge the following people without whom this book would have not been possible: Alfred Ricci, who devotedly worked on the manuscript over a ten-year period before entrusting it to my editor. I declare my boundless gratitude to the universe for delivering my empathic miracle editor, Anita Rehker. With deepest gratitude I thank my dear friends John and Rikka whose faith in my message led them to introduce me to my publisher. To Zhena Muzyka and Simon & Schuster, I am beyond humbled that you would take this project under your wing and bring a lifetime's dream to fruition. And to our superb developmental editor, Emily Han, goes my deep appreciation for her heartfelt work and commitment to the publication of this book.

It is an honor to be so supported by so many exemplary individuals, and I am most grateful to all of them. In particular I thank Dr. Michael Bernard Beckwith for his spiritual friendship and for welcoming me into his spiritual family at the Agape International Spiritual Center; Ellen and Garry, whom I met some thirty years ago at their spiritual center, which led to our serving together these many years; Melinda and Orville, whose dedication to selfless service has been such an inspiration to me throughout our friendship; to Judy goes my profound gratitude for being unflaggingly supportive at the outset of my profession; and immeasurable gratitude to Ned for forty-five years of believing in me and my work, which has made so many things possible.

To my cherished friend and most avid supporter Gayle goes my thanks for unconditionally being at my side; Nancy for her positive spirit and all the years we've been there for each other; and a very special acknowledgment to Alexandra, my lifelong friend who never fails to keep me on the course of my deepest purpose.

To every client and student with whom I have had the blessing of coming in contact, I offer my heartfelt love and gratitude for having trusted me with the most intimate, vulnerable, and precious aspects of your lives. While your names have been changed to protect your privacy, your stories are the very soul of this book.

Before spirit and my lifelong guides, I can only bend a knee in wordless gratitude for their guiding presence on every page of this book.

—HANS C. KING

Appendix A:
Frequently Asked Questions

THROUGHOUT ALL MY years of working with clients, I've observed a commonality in the questions asked before, during, and after a session. The loss of a loved one, an animal companion, receiving a medical prognosis of one's own impending death, getting a shock wave of unexpected news that causes a crumbling into inner chaos, validating a message or visitation from the spirit world, discovering one's child has an invisible playmate—these are just some examples of what brings a person to seek out the services of a medium. And when that appointment is made, clients have important questions relevant not only to issues related to their past, present, and future, but also about the process of working with a medium.

For me, a client's questions prior to our session serve as insightful indicators for entering a care-filled conversation about the vulnerability, intimacy, and integrity of the sacred, co-creative journey we will be taking together. Questions asked during a session are valuable contributors to establishing an energy of increasing openness, receptivity, and mutual trust between the client, myself, and the spirit world. At the close of my transmission from the spirit world, clients' questions provide me with intuitive insights into how I can best support them in metabolizing and working with the reading's contents in a spirit of loving kindness, patience, and compassion toward themselves once they are in the aloneness of their own company.

On the pages that follow, I share with you some of those questions, some of which perhaps arose in your own mind while reading a specific book chapter. Or maybe there was a time in your life when you considered seeing a reader but weren't sure how to select one that would best suit your purpose, thus preventing or postponing your having done so. Let me assure you that it's never too late for you to give yourself permission to demystify life events or validate your own intuitive insights, whether they involve yourself, the people with whom you currently share your life, or the lives of departed loved ones.

May the questions and answers that follow offer encouragement to your heart, peace to your mind, and nourishment to your spirit.

Must I myself believe in the possibility of communicating with those in the spirit world in order for a reading to come through in a session with a medium?

Whatever your personal beliefs are at this point in your life's journey, they have no impact on the transmission of communication from the spirit world through a medium. Fortunately for us all, life's ultimate truths are not dependent upon our belief in them for their existence.

Since seeking the services of a medium is against my religion, would this affect the reading I receive? My departed loved ones were also in the same religion, so would this impact their receptivity to my reaching out to them through a medium?

While a conflict between your faith tradition and your personal choice to consult with a medium cannot affect the reading itself, it can result in how you approach and respond to the reading which may include, for example, feelings such as guilt, resistance, doubt, or confusion. However, here is some encouraging news for you: More than once I have experienced a client's "conversion in consciousness," if you will, caused by a reading which was so accurate, so precise from the greatest to the smallest detail, there was no room for the client to deny or doubt the presence of the loved one who came forward and the message that was transmitted.

Now, when it comes to a loved one's religious beliefs and practices while they were on the Earth plane, bear in mind that upon reaching the spirit world they continue to participate in an ever-evolving process of inner spiritual exploration, discovery, and growth. Free at last from the weight of dogmatism or belief in sin and punishment, they rejoice in the realization of their true nature and the unconditional love of spirit, which always has and ever shall accompany their journey in all realms of existence.

It's quite likely that during a reading with your loved ones in the spirit world, you will find that they are enthusiastic to share with you their new spiritual explorations and discoveries, as well as serving as your guides on your own journey, reassuring you all the way that you are cherished beyond what you can imagine.

Is there a difference in the clarity or potency of having a session with a medium in person, by phone, or on the Internet through Skype or FaceTime?

There is no separation between souls, regardless of their physical distance from one another on the earthly plane, or the illusion of distance between the earthly realm and the spirit world. We all share an unbroken energetic connection, independent of location. Therefore, whether a session is conducted in person, by phone, or on the Internet, in no way is the clarity or accuracy of the medium's reading affected.

It is also true that each client is unique in nature, enabling some to be more focused, at ease, open, and receptive when their reading is conducted in person, while for others it makes no difference at all. The main point is that there is no right or wrong, better or worse, where location or communication technology is concerned.

I speak from experience when I say that the spirit world communicates with equal precision under all circumstances—there is absolutely no static interference relative to spatial configuration.

During a session, does the medium communicate only with my departed family members or loved ones from my current lifetime? Or do spirits I didn't meet in this incarnation or don't remember from other lifetimes also show up with messages for me? And how does this apply to my spirit guides?

An authentic medium's consciousness is an open and receptive space through which communication occurs but is not limited to: departed family members, including those who made their transition to the spirit world prior to the client's own birth; a client's child who may have died during the birthing process, a miscarriage, or abortion; loved ones and acquaintances; spirit-souls from this and prior lifetimes who have communication to transmit relevant to the client's questions and concerns; and master guides and spirit guides who are assigned to assisting an individual's evolutionary progress.

Spirit-souls who show up during a reading can also just as likely have been our spiritual teachers from a past life, individuals whose paths we crossed for a brief time, or those who wish to make amends with us about events from lifetimes we no longer recall. I must also add that there have been instances when a client hadn't yet heard about a friend's or relative's death who came forth with a message for me to deliver. Another possibility involves role reversal, meaning that the parts we play in each other's lives shift around in different lifetimes, so those who may have been our students in another life come forward as our teachers in the spirit world, as well as other relational configurations such as parents and children.

Thank goodness that in spirit's wisdom we cannot recall all of our lifetimes and their details until we're evolved enough to handle what is revealed!

It is important to understand that the relationships in our lives are far beyond the human definitions we use to describe them as well as how we relate to them. In our three-dimensional realm, human relationships are described primarily in legal terms, which are used for the purpose of creating an organized, controlled society. In contrast, our relational connections from a spiritual reference point are far more expansive and profound than what can be described in mere words.

Some of my family and friends on the other side never learned to speak English. Do I need to work with a medium who speaks their languages—Spanish and Hebrew?

The spirit world speaks the one universal language of Divine Love, which translates just perfectly into the language spoken by the medium and client.

Is there a specific length of time I should wait following the recent passing of my sister before making an appointment to communicate with her through a medium?

I want you to know that yours is a very loving, unselfish, considerate question to ask. While there are commonalities we all share in the process of transitioning to our new dimension of living, there are also aspects that are unique to each individual spirit-soul, one of which includes the length of time required for acclimating to the energetic frequency of the spirit world. Once acclimated, a spirit's accessibility and receptivity to being approached by a medium and loved one from the earthly realm increases.

It may be helpful to you if I share what was once told to me by one of my own guides. Individuals who are literally catapulted out of their human form through a car accident, a war, or airplane crash—to name a few tragic examples—experience shock when suddenly finding themselves being escorted by spirit guides into an unfamiliar realm of existence. Although immense love accompanies them, even for the most evolved and courageous of souls, it remains an unexpected transition. Likewise, in the case of suicide, it may take a person a little more time to make an unanticipated energetic adjustment due to the suddenness of arriving in an entirely new vibratory realm.

The understanding to take away here is that although the measurement of what we call "time" is vastly different in the spirit world than in our three-dimensional realm, there is an energetic "time-correlation" we all pass through when transitioning to the spirit world. The good news is we have the benefit of loving, understanding, and compassionate spirits as our personal escorts throughout the process.

Your question also invites us to consider a client's own readiness to receive communication from a loved one who has recently transitioned to the spirit world. Although it is completely natural to want to know how a departed loved one is doing, to reunite and receive a comforting message from them, if the client is immersed in intense grief and is crying to the point of distraction, receptivity to the medium's reading may be affected. While it is certainly appropriate and even expected by the medium that the client will have tears to shed during the session, if the client's grief is so overwhelming that it continuously disrupts the session, the medium may compassionately suggest that a later appointment would better serve the desired results.

Since the purpose of having a session with a medium is for healing and bringing peace to the heart where a departed loved one is concerned, it is the higher part of wisdom to be somewhat beyond the earliest stages of the grieving process which, as earlier mentioned, varies from individual to individual. When a client is in doubt as to which stage of grief he is in and finds himself spending a great deal of time in gut-wrenching tears, my practice is to recommend seeing a professional grief counselor prior to having a session with a medium.

Bear in mind also that because your departed loved ones are aware of and sensitive to your current state of consciousness, they may choose to postpone communicating until they know you are ready to be receptive to their presence and messages.

Can a medium guarantee that a specific person I want to communicate with will come through?

While a medium can initiate contact with the individual the client wishes to connect with, it remains the prerogative of that spirit-soul to determine whether or not the communication will take place on that specific occasion. For reasons known to that individual, it may be considered wise to first seek guidance from one of her own guides before communicating, or to determine if it would be in the highest interest of all concerned to postpone communicating. (And no authentic medium will or can demand that a spirit come forth and participate in a session.) For the most part, it has been my experience that spirit-souls graciously respond to the medium's invitation and are very pleased to reconnect with their loved one whether or not they choose to convey a message in that particular session or a later one.

Is it possible for a medium to communicate with my dog, Sadie? I recently had to euthanize her due to old age and my heart longs to know that she is OK.

Animals have spirits, too, and it is absolutely possible for a medium to make contact with a beloved animal companion who has passed on. As well, I've conducted sessions where the spirit of a pet has come forward to deliver an unsolicited message to a client, as well as revealing that Fido had incarnated with his human companion throughout several lifetimes, albeit in different animal bodies. How comforting to know that we don't lose our connection to our beloved animal companions who love and serve us so unconditionally.

What is the difference between a psychic and a medium, and the kind of readings they give?

A medium has the ability to receive clairaudient messages from the spirit world with the utmost accuracy, free from interference by his human limitations. While mediums convey communication word for word as it is received from the spirit world, they do not interpret what is received, nor do they make use of external tools for their readings.

Psychics tune into their clairsentient ability and relay to the client their interpretation of what they intuit. They may also use tools such as Tarot cards, a crystal ball, tea leaves, runes, etc., during a reading.

Another important distinction is that mediums are always psychic, but psychics are not always mediums.

Is a medium positioned higher on the readership totem than a psychic?

The real question is not about hierarchy, but rather the type of reading desired by the client. For example, since a medium's specialty is to communicate messages directly from the spirit world to the client, this would be the viable choice for those wanting to communicate with departed family members and others. And while mediums are also psychic—which means you may ask questions about the various aspects of your life—a psychic may also be consulted in such matters.

Fundamentally, it is the client who determines the category of reader that best suits his current need, which can be determined by researching the various categories of readers on the Internet, at a library, or bookstore.

If a medium is famous, does that mean he or she is more qualified to give an accurate reading than less famous mediums?

When it comes to mediums, fame and accuracy are not necessarily synonyms. In fact, if a medium's ego gets seduced by name and fame, it can become a stumbling block. That being said, some of my famous colleagues have maintained their humility because they well know that spirit is the true doer, while they are simply its instrument. My personal relationship to my mediumship practice is grounded in the realization that the channel is blessed by the spirit that flows through it.

How do I go about selecting an ethical medium?

Do your due diligence! I cannot emphasize enough how vital it is to ask for referrals from those you know and whose assessments you can trust concerning their sessions with a medium. One important question to ask is if the medium paused during the reading to check in with the client, to see if what was coming through resonated with their intuitive perception. The underlying purpose for my recommending this is that a bona fide medium will always give you back to yourself, will self-empower you and consider your own intuitive perceptions relevant feedback during the session. It cannot be overemphasized that an ethical medium will never permit a client to become dependent upon him. The relationship between medium and client is not a co-dependent one, but rather a co-creative one.

Now, if you don't have family members or friends who have

had sessions with a medium, you can turn to the Internet for researching mediums, their qualifications, and personal testimonials from those with whom the medium has had sessions. By visiting their websites you will be able to view links that show a schedule of their upcoming events such as speaking engagements, classes, or workshops you may attend in person or by live stream to get a sense of how they resonate with you. You can also check their online archives for any past television appearances, video clips, radio shows, magazine interviews, etc. Look at any videos and photographs posted on their site and trust your intuition about the energy you pick up. Note also if their website is professionally presented.

The purpose for which I teach intuitive development courses is so students can learn how to cultivate and apply their innate intuitive faculty in the details of their everyday lives, including as a means for evaluating a reader and sensing if they feel a "click" within their own intuitive awareness. If you identify a medium whom you intuitively sense communicates with the spirit world in a consciousness of integrity and accuracy, you can feel confident in arranging a session.

Bear in mind that clients have the same responsibility for bringing their best to this co-creative relationship. By that I mean, for example, not "testing" a medium with dishonest statements to see if he/she can "catch you" and thereby prove to you that they are authentic. In other words, it's a waste of the medium's abilities and your money to play games. As well, I've observed that some individuals go from medium to medium until they receive the reading that provides the answers they *want to receive* rather than authentic guidance that the ego resists accepting, thus defeating the purpose of having a session in the first place.

These are some of the wisdom-guided ways you may establish an ethical ground for working with a reader in any category and fulfilling the purpose for which you desire their services, as well as how you as a client contribute to a mutually beneficial relationship with a reader.

Once having selected a medium, what is the most effective way to prepare myself for a session?

First, understand that it's quite natural to feel a spectrum of mindsets and emotions, which can include nervousness, self-consciousness, or vacillations about your decision prior to and up until the beginning of your session. This may be especially true if it is the first time you're experiencing a session with a medium or any category of reader. Second, you can rely on the fact that a medium is well aware of this natural human predicament and will gently support you in working through it.

Approximately an hour to thirty minutes before the time of your appointment, stop and enter a state of inner relaxation through meditation, prayer, deep breathing, a warm bath—whatever it is that escorts you into a place of inner quietude, openness, and receptivity. Again, because it's natural to be nervous, especially in your first session with a reader, avoid having that glass of wine, a toke of medical cannabis, or just slightly more of a pain prescription—even a homeopathic one—in an attempt to calm your jitters.

A colleague of mine once shared an experience where a client who had never before seen a medium and had doubts about whether mediumship was real or not, humorously confessed after the session to having made a "pre-session agreement" with a loved one in the spirit world about a "sign" that would be "proof" that the reading was indeed authentic. Much to the client's delight, even though the sign he single-mindedly designed did not manifest, the reading he received far surpassed his expectations. The moral of this story is to enter a session knowing that once you have done your due diligence in selecting a medium, there is nothing more required than an open mind and heart.

How much information should I be prepared to provide the medium about the loved ones in the spirit world with whom I want to communicate? Is it different if I want to talk about a person who is still in the human form?

Concerning individuals in the spirit world with whom you want the medium to communicate, only very basic information such as their name and relationship to you is required. More is not necessary, as it is customary for your loved one to offer any additional information that is relevant to the session.

When it comes to having a session about someone who is still in human form, in addition to providing a name, you may describe to the medium their relationship to you along with the specific questions you have. As well, you may invite others to attend your session. If, for example, your daughter has informed you that she talks with an invisible friend, it is your choice as to whether you include her in your first session so that relevant questions/issues can arise and be addressed. In some circumstances, depending upon the information you conveyed when making your appointment, the medium may recommend not including anyone else in a first session and instead bringing them in at a later time.

Can spirit guides who aren't family members or loved ones also support me with a specific challenge, finding a new job, finances, and relationships?

Absolutely. As mentioned earlier, spirits on the other side are given assignments by their own guides based on their areas of specialization, which means that their job description includes guiding those on the Earth plane who would benefit from their expertise. When these spirit guides come through in sessions with my clients, they give their name and communicate their guidance in response to the client's questions. I encourage clients to be receptive to them not only during our sessions, but also to call on them throughout any given day when desiring guidance. Spirit guides will answer through the client's intuitive faculty or through the synchronicities that occur in life's everyday circumstances.

Do I have the same spirit guides throughout my lifetime?

Not necessarily, but new ones will make their presence known either through a medium or your own intuition. In either circumstance, ask for their name, and if one doesn't come through, assign them one because they will answer to it.

Why are some people born with the ability to sense guidance from the spirit world and others are not?

We are all equipped with the sixth sense of intuition, but it is up to us to consciously invest the effort and discipline to discover and cultivate it. Those who appear to have been "born" with the ability to intuitively sense guidance have cultivated their intuitive faculty perhaps throughout many incarnations, so it accompanies them in their karmic birth suitcase when they reincarnate on the Earth plane. Know for certain that there is no reason to be discouraged if you don't sense guidance at this time because just as with any other skill, the more you use your intuition the more finely tuned it becomes. Go for it!

This may be an awkward question, but I'm going to ask it anyway. Do our guides watch everything we do in life, like during intimate activities such as having sex?

You would be surprised to know how many times I am asked this very question! Our guides are not voyeurs and certainly honor our privacy in all matters. The source of a question such as yours is rooted in religious dogma that believes in an anthropomorphic god whose omnipresent eye is vigilantly watching over and judging every detail of our lives from whether we brush our teeth after every meal, whether we cheated on our income tax, when and with whom we're having sex, to what we put in the church collection basket. You can relax in the assurance that neither our Creator Source, our loved ones in the spirit world, nor our guides concern themselves with such issues, nor are they Peeping Toms.

Why is it that I can sometimes intuitively hear my guides very clearly while at other times—even when I most need it—I can't hear them at all?

When you experience inner static caused by such things as mind chatter, anxiety, restlessness, stress, or an invasive physical challenge, your intuitive antenna weakens, affecting your reception to guidance from the spirit world. That's the time to take a break, breathe deeply, take a warm bath, meditate—whatever it is that relaxes and reinvigorates you. And remember, your guides will know when your antenna is once again crackling with receptivity and they will be near at hand to communicate with you. Your part is to create an inner fertile field for receiving it.

Why is my intuition clearer when I apply it to supporting others, but less clear when I want to access it to help myself?

The answer is similar to why a lawyer does not represent himself in court, a medical doctor does not treat family members, why therapists have therapists, writers have editors, and mediums consult with their own personal guides. We human beings get in our own way through mind chatter and our attachment to what it tells us, which undermines our ability to receive intuitive guidance in support of ourselves. The prescription for getting out of our own way is to cultivate the qualities of nonattachment, surrender, trust, humility, and practice, practice, practice of letting go of our mind chatter and how we think things ought to be.

Does spirit involve itself with our use of free will?

Our Creator Source does not interfere with our free will. Nor does spirit judge, interfere, or take sides in man's inhumanity to man taking place throughout the three-dimensional world. Rather, the impersonal laws governing the universe very efficiently handle the cause-and-effect results of the choices and actions made on both the individual level and the collective consciousness of humanity.

I'm quite confident in saying that spirit must get a kick out of the continuing theological debates over free will versus predestination. Regardless of the metaphysical concepts, cherished religious convictions, or existential beliefs that we cling to, our existence in the third dimension contains many mysteries and paradoxes, and when we learn how to accept and make peace with them, we are on our way to becoming a spiritual adult.

How can we human beings remain more consciously connected to spirit's presence throughout our daily activities?

On a daily basis dive into the depths of your soul and drink the blissful ambrosia of communion with spirit through your inner spiritual practices of meditation and contemplative prayer. Then watch how their aftereffects support you in maintaining a conscious connection to spirit's presence and guidance whether you are standing at the kitchen sink, delivering a financial report in your workplace, or sitting in quiet repose. This is what the mystical lovers and knowers of spirit across all spiritual traditions practice and teach their students, because it works.

Appendix B:
Bonus Spirit Guide
and Client Stories

I SHARE WITH you here several more stories culled from my client archives. Upon revisiting those stretching back even as far as fifty-five years, I still gain new insights from what my clients have taught me and feel tremendously blessed for having been invited to participate in their lives in such a personally meaningful way. I hope their stories will likewise be a source of encouragement and upliftment to you.

This first section of stories is related to families and children, and is followed by a selection of animal companion stories.

The Healing Reunion of a Beloved Clan

Having made a soul agreement in the spirit world, Bonnie and Susan entered the three-dimensional realm as fraternal twins. Sadly, just seven short years later, Bonnie returned to the other side when her doctor was unable to save her from pneumonia's grip.

Susan immediately went into a downward spiral of depression, resulting in weight loss and performing poorly in school. During some of her crying spells, Susan's parents would overhear her scolding Bonnie for leaving her stranded and accusing her of taking away the other half of herself.

Life was not unfolding according to how Susan remembered hers and Bonnie's prebirth pact, which my guides told me is not an untypical side effect of entering the vibratory density of the Earth plane, where memories of agreements made on the other side begin to diminish as "humanness" takes root in our consciousness.

In response to the tireless efforts Susan's parents made at consoling and communicating with her, Susan's intense grief resulted in one consistent response: "You don't understand! Half of me went to heaven with Bonnie, and it can't come back."

A few weeks later, when Diane and Phil were out having dinner with friends who had known the girls since birth, they shared with them Susan's tremendous difficulty in adjusting to the loss of her sister. The wife, Beverly, fully empathizing with Diane and Phil, shared with them that she and her husband, Jason, had a few sessions with me following the passing of their son, and that perhaps all three of them—Diane, Phil, and Susan—might also find solace from a reading. Beverly gave them my telephone number and Diane scheduled a session for the following week.

On Diane and Phil's first visit to my Miami office, Susan did not accompany them. They felt she was still a little too raw to predict how she would respond to what might unfold during my reading. As well, they wanted to share some background details outside of Susan's hearing. Toward the end of our session, I let them know the spirit world said Susan was now ready to join us. They were overjoyed when I delivered Bonnie's message that she, too, would be there to speak to them and comfort Susan by reminding her of the agreements they had made on the other side.

Four days later the family arrived for our appointment. As Phil led Susan toward their seats, I noticed that her right hand was clutching a piece of paper against her chest, directly over her heart. Even after she sat down, Susan's hand remained in the same position.

"Did you bring something to show me?" I gently asked her.

Without turning around the piece of paper for me to see, Susan responded, "I brought my sister Bonnie with me. She used to go everywhere with me. But then she went to heaven without me. So now I take her picture with me everywhere I go, cuz it's kind of like she's still here with me."

"Bonnie *is* with you, sweetheart," I assured her. "And you know what, she's telling me to tell you that she still has the red barrettes that each of you got on your fifth birthday from your mom and dad. She wants you to know she wears them all the time with her red-and-white polka-dot dress."

Susan's eyes grew large, affirming the facts I had just communicated. She immediately rose from her seat, ran over to me, and handed me the piece of paper she had been holding over her heart. And there was Bonnie, smiling up at me and wearing red barrettes, which held her blond pigtails in place.

"Does she talk to you? Please tell her I miss her so much! Will she answer you? Why does she talk to you and not to me?" Susan pleaded, her voice cracking as tears poured down her little pink cheeks.

What a joy that Bonnie had begun to come through so immediately in response to her sister's plaintive cry! "Bonnie is telling me right now that she has never left you, Susan, that she is right by your side, even when you're asleep, and that she will send messages to you, and your mom and dad."

Then, to my utter delight, a spirit guide assigned to Bonnie and Susan since their birth made her presence known in the reading.

"And that's not all, Susan," I continued. "You and Bonnie still have the same spirit angel who is watching over you both. She's with us right now. [At this juncture, I didn't know who was weeping more—Phil or Diane.]

"You're really going to like this good news. Bonnie is telling me that the doctor you just saw who said you're going to have to wear glasses for the rest of your life is wrong. You'll only be wearing them for a couple of years." The look of relief on Susan's face said it all!

The three of us ended the session encircled in spirit's grace.

In our next session, to which Phil and Diane also brought Susan, a most surprising revelation came through, one which the parents had never previously disclosed, not even during our private sessions.

"Before we talk about how the results of our last session are unfolding," I said in an effort to prepare them for what was to come, "right now I'm being told to share what came through spirit the moment you stepped in the door."

After Phil and Diane sat down directly across from me, as sensitively as was humanly possible, I said, "Spirit is telling me that you lost two children a few years before the twins were born." Their complexions simultaneously took on an ashen hue. Being the first to collect himself, Phil said, "Yes, we did. A son and a daughter."

"I lost my son in childbirth," Diane echoed in barely a whisper, "and our daughter drowned when she was four."

"Well, it's my joy to tell you your son and daughter are now both standing right in front of your chairs, with beautiful smiles spread across their faces, asking me to tell you that they love you very much and thank you for having been the vehicles that brought them into the world."

Suddenly, the floodgates of their hearts opened, sending a silent torrent of tears down Phil's and Diane's faces, releasing the residue of agony that they had been suppressing over the loss of their two beloved children. Susan sat quietly at their side, sensing the palpable momentousness of the moment. Although I normally share such revelations with parents privately, I was told by spirit that there was a deep soul-bond among all six members of this dear family and that now was the right time for them to be reunited.

Susan was the first to speak. "I have a brother and sister who are here with us? And we're all together—is Bonnie here, too?"

I don't know who was more elated—Phil, Diane, or Susan—to know that the spirits of Bonnie and the other two children were thriving in the spirit world while continuing to be accessible to them from the Earth plane.

Susan didn't let Bonnie off the hook quite as easily as her parents did. She wanted to know why, if Bonnie had always been at her side, she had kept the existence of their siblings a secret from her.

"Well, sweetheart," I began, "it wasn't that Bonnie was

keeping it a secret. In the spirit world our guides tell us when the time is right for sharing things with our loved ones on Earth. And even though you and Bonnie never met your brother and sister while you were together in the spirit world, she told me they helped her cross over when she died, and that's when they told her who they were. When she asked them why neither of you got to meet them on the other side, they told her that if they had introduced themselves then, you and Bonnie would have postponed your birth on Earth. They are as happy as you and Bonnie are to be together today, and to reconnect with your mom and dad."

When they returned home that evening, Diane and Phil showed Susan photographs of her deceased sister Katie. When Susan indicated one of Katie's photos was her favorite, they let her cut out Katie's face from it which she then placed across from Bonnie's photo in a locket she always wore. As the years passed, Susan found it very comforting to journal about her ongoing communication with her loved ones in the spirit world.

Needless to say, the entire family reveled in their reunion, and from that day on their lives were a continuous celebration of their beautiful, eternal bond.

It's sessions such as these that metaphorically bring me to my knees in gratitude to be a channel of such heart-healing, spirit-lifting communication from the spirit world. And I can't overstate how my soul sings whenever I meet parents who tenderly and selflessly support their children by trusting in their communication with loved ones on the other side.

Even the Spirit World Uses
Props to Make a Point

For thirty years, through sleet and snow, I conducted sessions in Manhattan. One day a client, Julie, called to inform me she was sending over a couple to see me about their eldest son, Jeffrey, who had crossed over to the other side. Since they were already on their way from her apartment, I was grateful that a 4:00 PM appointment slot—the last of the day—had become available due to a cancellation.

As soon as the couple stepped across the threshold of my office door, with my inner eye I saw a red baseball cap fly across the room. Well, I certainly wasn't going to make that a public service announcement upon shaking hands and exchanging introductions with Trudy and Jake. So I simply parked the vision of the red cap in my mind as having possible relevance to our session. But only for mere seconds.

Immediately upon sitting down, Jake began waving his hands as though he were pushing an unwelcome kitten from his lap. "How odd," he quizzically exclaimed with eyebrows furrowed. "Something just landed on my lap. I felt the weight of it. Is that normal in these kinds of . . . uh?"

"Medium sessions," I said, making my best attempt at diplomatically filling in the blanks, fatigued as I was after a full day of sessions. Then, not having the benefit of what was yet to be revealed, I rather impulsively added, "Well, it might have been that red baseball cap that flew across the room in Spirit's attempt at being humorous!"

Trudy gasped, Jake immediately broke into tears, while

I froze in place waiting for an explanation of what had just happened.

Having a bit more control in the moment than her husband, Trudy began sharing that they had lost their eldest son, Jeffrey, who, since the age of three, had worn a red baseball cap which his father gave him every year on his birthday. She described how Jeff wore his cap everywhere, the shower and swimming pool being the only exceptions to his personal rule. "Jake kept all eighteen of them, even the ones he'd outgrown," she said with great affection.

"And there was never a problem with Jeff wearing the cap to school," Jake added, "until that phone call came from Jeff's high school principal, Mr. Jenkins, who stiffly informed us, 'Jeffrey's wardrobe accessory simply isn't acceptable.' "

Trudy further explained how Jeffrey and his parents were called to Mr. Jenkins's office for a meeting, during which the principal explained that every time a teacher asked that Jeffrey remove his baseball cap during class his adamant response was "You don't understand! I can't do my classwork without my hat."

"Although the principal preferred another outcome," Trudy continued, "he finally gave up, based on the fact that Jeffrey's senior year would be over very shortly, putting an end to what he called 'the baseball cap addiction.' " [As an aside, Jeff never shared the root cause of his attachment to the cap, so beyond sentimental purposes, we let it go as having given him some sense of inner security.]

"During the Thanksgiving break in his freshman year of college"—Jake had now picked up the thread of the story—"we sent Jeff a plane ticket home for the holidays. From the airport he got a shuttle, and on the way home a drunk driver rammed into it. When we arrived at the hospital, we were told that Jeff was pronounced dead upon arrival. All we had left with was his suitcase, backpack, and baseball cap.

"Jake took it so hard he had to extend his bereavement leave from work," Trudy elaborated. "He and Jeff had a very loving, deep father-son relationship from the day Jeff came into the world until he left."

At that precise juncture, Jeffrey made his presence known to me. Considering the rawness of his parents' emotional state, I slowly and softly informed them, "Jeffrey is here with us now, and wants to first say something to you, Jake."

Taking his cue, Jeffrey jumped right in. "Please stop your suicidal thoughts!" he sternly admonished Jake.

Understandably, Trudy's face paled and, turning to her husband, she said, "What? You would leave me to raise our two beautiful sons without you?"

"The pain of having lost Jeffrey haunts me, practically tortures me day and night," Jake wailed.

I raised my hand, indicating we should pause, because Jeffrey had more to say to his father. "If you commit suicide, I'm here to tell you that you would inflict the same tremendous grief on Mom and my two brothers that you have suffered over losing me. And I know you love them too much to have them suffer like that!"

Immediately, Jake profusely apologized first to Trudy, and next to Jeffrey.

Then, speaking directly to his son, he said, "Now I understand why the red baseball cap came into the room at the same time we did. It was proof that you have been with us all along, that you are not really dead, taken from us forever as I had thought you were. When the cap fell on my lap, it was you who threw it at me, to sit there just like you did when you were a little boy. Those were some of the most beautiful moments of my life."

"Yes, Dad," Jeffrey confirmed, "for me as well, and even though I grew out of sitting on your lap, I've still never left your side, Mom's side, or my brothers' sides. Remember these words: I will come for you when you cross over, but it won't be for a long time, because neither you nor Mom are leaving the family anytime soon. Besides, my little brothers will need you to babysit the seven grandchildren they are going to bring into the world!"

Expect the Unexpected

Olivia and Art arranged a private session with me when their son Jaime was seven years old and a serious illness nearly claimed his life. One day, while sitting at Jaime's hospital bedside, he authoritatively announced to his parents, "My friend Michael told me I'm not going to die now."

After exchanging glances with Olivia, Art asked his son to repeat what he had just said.

"Well, Michael came to me last night and told me that you're going to be taking me home from the hospital real soon because it's not my time to die," Jaime reiterated.

His parents told me they were shocked into silence by Jaime's statement, because Jaime had never met his older brother, Michael, who had died some years before he was born. In fact, they never told Jaime they had a child prior to his birth, nor were there any photos placed around the house that would cause Jaime to ask any questions. Instead, they agreed that when they felt the time was right they would tell him, but as far as they were concerned, that day had not yet arrived. Obviously, Michael knew this and, respecting their wishes, didn't introduce himself to Jaime as being his older brother, leaving him with the belief that he was a trustworthy friend who lived in the spirit world, a fact which Jaime unquestionably and happily accepted.

It came to pass that Michael's earlier statement that Jaime would not die "now" meant that his life would be extended for only two additional years, leaving his parents brokenhearted at now having lost two beloved sons. We continued to have sessions during which, to Olivia's and Art's joy, both Jaime and Michael continued to offer their guiding presence.

During the years when we had no sessions, Olivia and Art had another son, Jose. One day, when Jose was about six, the family was on their way to visit some friends when Jose said, "My brother said to turn left, and after the stop sign to go four blocks and turn right," resulting in Olivia giving me an on-the-spot call from her cell phone to make an appointment.

Four days later, our session picked up where Olivia's phone call left off, with Art taking the lead.

"When Jose used the word 'brother' it didn't register with me. I didn't take it literally because I thought he was just interjecting himself into the casual conversation Olivia and I were having. So, playing along with him, I said, 'Your brother sure knows his way around, because that's exactly the direction where we're headed!' "

Art further shared that he didn't connect the dots that linked their present circumstances to those of the past, when Jaime first met Michael.

Jose, however, had succeeded in catching Olivia's attention, causing her to ask him, "Well, if he's really your brother, wouldn't your father and I know him?"

"Jaime's an *invisible* brother who lives somewhere in heaven, not on Earth, so you don't know him," Jose clarified for her. "He comes to visit me when I'm in bed at night. Last week Jaime told me we're going to move from our house and I felt kind of sad."

Olivia confirmed to me that she and Art had been having discussions about moving, but never in Jose's presence.

"As you know from our sessions with Jaime, we accepted what he told us about Michael," Olivia explained. "But for something like that to repeat itself with Jose, we were so flabbergasted we wanted to see you right away to find out what's going on. We want to support our beautiful son. We feel so blessed that he has come into our life and we couldn't bear losing him. Sometimes we're afraid that Jaime—or even Michael—will tell Jose or us that he has come to escort Jose to the spirit world. Jose might be fine receiving that news, but I don't think Art and I could handle it. Even though we know we're always connected, we don't want to lose the joys of a tangible, face-to-face relationship with our son."

I shared with them Jaime's message of assurance that Jose would be with them throughout their years on the planet, that he would not only continue to be one of the spirit guides to all three of them, he would also be present at the time each one of them passed over to the spirit world. (Eventually, in later sessions, Michael also introduced himself to Jose and told him that he was his older brother. To the relief of us all, Jose was thrilled with the news.)

But an even greater surprise from the other side awaited the family when, one morning during breakfast, Jose excitedly announced to his parents, "Last night Jaime told me I'm going to have a baby sister!" As you might imagine, this generated an immediate call from Olivia for a private reading for her and Art!

"Well," Olivia leaned toward me and confided during our session, "this is the first time Art and I doubted that Jose received Jaime's message accurately, because years earlier I'd had a medical procedure that greatly reduced, if not entirely eliminated, the possibility of me getting pregnant."

With eyebrows raised, I enigmatically smiled at Olivia and Art as though to say, "Well, we'll just see about that," all the while sending a cosmic wink to Jaime in the spirit world.

Three years later, Art and Olivia made an appointment to introduce me to their beautiful baby daughter and Jose's little sister, Isabel.

Randy Meets Silver Birch

Some years ago, Cecelia and Richard came to my Miami Beach office for a session about their son, Randy, whom I'd known since his birth. At the age of twelve, Randy began having visitations from a Native American elder who introduced himself as Silver Birch.

When Randy enthusiastically shared with his parents the guidance he received from Silver Birch, they were concerned he might have a mental disorder. The doctor to whom they took Randy wanted to run some tests on his brain to determine if he was having hallucinations, or if he was partially autistic, and therefore unable to properly express what might have been a normal dream in language that was understandable to them. It was while they were taking some time to consider the doctor's recommendation that Randy tired of his parents treating him like a victim. "I don't want to live if this is how my life is going to be," he informed them. Quite naturally, the possibility of Randy attempting to end his life terrified them, so they made an immediate appointment to see me.

"How do we decide in which direction to go to best help our son, Hans?" they implored. When I asked them to share examples of how they communicated with Randy when he shared his visitations from Silver Birch, it was easy to see that fear and lack of understanding dominated their conversations with him. Now, it was quite another thing when they requested sessions with me for readings over the years, but when it came to their son directly receiving messages from the spirit world it was beyond their capacity to imagine him as being a candidate for such a clairvoyant experience. When I suggested they bring Randy to our next session, they agreed.

As soon as the family sat down across from me, a striking Native American gentleman came forward. He stood near Randy, silently observing. I understood from this that it was not the moment to announce his presence, so instead I informed Randy that we were having a session to hear from him about his relationship with his Native American friend.

"A tall, dark Indian man who wears a feather in his hair told me I'm not sick, that there's nothing wrong with me," Randy spluttered. "He said I'm sensitive to energy patterns and that makes me a little different from other children. But not in a bad way. He usually visits me at night, just before I fall asleep, but this morning he surprised me and told me, 'You are on your right path. You just walk on a different side of the street than other children. All is well.' "

We adults remained quiet. Randy picked up the thread of his story saying, "I ask Silver Birch questions when he comes to me, like why he visits me and other things, and he always says, 'We will put the answer in your heart.' And I don't exactly know how it happens, but I do get answers, sometimes when Silver Birch is still standing near my bed, and sometimes later on, I concentrate on my heart and get an answer."

At that point I handed Randy a pad and pencil and asked him to draw a picture of the Native American. He drew a picture of a man with a feather in his hair under which he wrote, "I no longer am afraid." I was amazed at the precise likeness between the picture Randy drew and Silver Birch, still standing close by listening to all that was being said.

Sensing the time was now right, I said, "Silver Birch is with us. He looks just like your drawing, Randy, and he's telling me that you are destined to continue drawing and writing, just as you did now." Immediately, a look of relief spread not only across Randy's face, but the faces of his parents. Since that time, with the loving support of Cecelia and Richard, Randy confidently continued to draw images and write a one-sentence line containing a teaching of Silver Birch under each one.

Needless to say, from that point on Randy's parents opened their hearts and minds to his experiences, even requesting him to ask Silver Birch questions on their behalf. They were never disappointed in his responses!

Our Animal Companions

"Whenever I was properly humble and willing to let something besides a human be my instructor, these various four-legged, six-legged, and no-legged fellows shared priceless wisdom with me," wrote J. Allen Boone in his 1954 classic, *Kinship with All Life*.[1] Still in print, Boone touchingly describes his personal, unconventional relationships with many animal species from Strongheart, the all-time great motion picture dog-star, rattlesnakes, and worms to Freddy the fly. Never claiming his ability to be anything extraordinary, he credited his animal communication skills to the "perfect understanding and perfect co-operation between the human and all other forms of life . . . whenever the human really does his required part."

If we can allow ourselves to admit it, which of us has not confided in a treasured pet—either silently or out loud—our secret longings, fears, heartaches, and joys? Our pets somehow allow us to drop our self-consciousness, pride, embarrassment, and shame. When we share with a pet, our armor falls away and we become more open, more self-revealing, not just to Fido, but also to ourselves. And so it is that these beloved companions become so dear to us that we yearn for assurance that they are doing well and that we will be reunited with our "best friend."

It is my joy to tell you that whether little Lucky or Sparky are gracing the other side or have rejoined us once again on the Earth plane, there exists plenty of factual evidence of our unbroken connection to these treasured friends, and when the proper conditions are created, we can communicate with them in the universal language of love. I'd like to take this law of life a bit further by sharing with you some client sessions that introduce the essence and depth of our kinship with our beloved animal companions.

MABEL HARRINGTON THE
SECOND—*OR IS SHE?*

Mabel, an adorable black Labrador, was a deeply loved companion to Marjorie Harrington, a client of mine in her early eighties who lived in Hull, England. Marjorie came to the United States once or twice a year to visit her daughter, Jacqueline, and it was their custom to have a session or two with me during her stay.

Just under a year had passed since Marjorie visited the US, and I was so happy to receive a call from Jacqueline, her daughter, to arrange a session. Three days later they arrived at my studio office. In my enthusiasm to see them I couldn't get to the door fast enough, but as soon as I opened it and saw their faces, I knew. "Oh my goodness, you've lost your precious Mabel!" They wept all the way to their chairs. For Marjorie it was especially heartbreaking because she had raised Mabel from a puppy to the ripe age of seventeen, not to mention Mabel was a very major presence in her life since the passing of her beloved husband many years earlier.

Although I know full well it's not possible to dictate to the spirit world, I lifted my heart to my own spirit guide, to Mabel, and to Marjorie's husband hoping to receive guidance, or an update—whatever would take the edge off Marjorie's sorrow and Jacqueline's concern about her mother's grief.

All at once I heard a panting sound, followed by an awareness of Mabel's presence. I don't know who was happier—Marjorie, Jacqueline, or me—when I announced, "Mabel is here with us now and she wants to know, Marjorie, if you want her to return to you on the Earth plane."

"Of course I want her to come back, Hansie, and please tell her that. But I'm rather long in the tooth now and my shelf life is definitely getting closer to its expiration date! I'm not certain that I have the energy or mobility to care for her as I once did," she said in a melancholy tone. Mabel patiently sat by, transmitting to me an equally melancholy groan.

Not wanting to cause Marjorie further discomfort, we moved on to inviting Jonathan, her departed husband, into our circle. Jonathan was very pleased to be able to convey messages to both his wife and his daughter, including his heartfelt consolation over Marjorie's loss of Mabel. We met one more time before Marjorie returned to Hull.

Seven months had now passed and it was the time of year when Jacqueline traditionally spent a month in Hull visiting her mother. Upon her return to the US, after about two weeks of resting from her trip, her routine was to give me a call and let me know how Marjorie was doing. This time, however, she called after just four days and wanted a session as soon as possible.

"While Mom and I were out to lunch at an outdoor café with friends one afternoon, we heard a chorus of barking coming from a medium-sized box that was just a bit down from our table. You see," she explained, "in England it's customary for persons who have puppies for sale or to give away to place them in a box and stand alongside it at a street curb with the hope that passersby will be inclined to pick out one of the little darlings and take it home.

"Well, all of a sudden we noticed that the man who had been standing by the box was walking with very deliberate steps toward our table. Upon arrival he said, 'Excuse me, but I have your puppy.'

"Considering it a sales ploy I said, 'Thank you, sir, but this isn't a good time. We're not looking for a puppy.'

" 'Well,' he quipped, 'that isn't what the little six-pound, chocolate Labrador in the box told me. In fact, I hope you won't think me too bold when I tell you I've already named her for you: Mabel.'

"Hansie," she said, using her mother's term of affection for me, "there was only one thing my mother ever said she wanted to change about Mabel, which was she had wished she were brown!"

"Then what happened?" I asked like a wide-eyed child hanging on to her every word. The truth is, I was purposely suspending my own knowing of how the story was going to end because the joy of Jacqueline's telling of it was so endearing that I didn't want to give myself a spoiler alert!

"Well," she continued, "the man said, 'Mabel has already made up her mind that she's going home with you.' That was all Mom had to hear. Suddenly, she transformed right before my eyes, and with the strength of a fifty-year-old she picked up Mabel and sat her on her lap. Turning to the man who spoke on Mabel's behalf, Mom said, 'I shall rename her Mabel Harrington the Second, because she's my second Labrador named Mabel.' "

"Jacqueline, I need you to call your mother as soon as you get home and tell her this is not Mabel Harrington the Second," I instructed her. "It is indeed the spirit of Mabel the First reincarnated in this puppy. And that man was the spirit world's ambassador, reuniting them as was meant to be."

"You're absolutely right," Jacqueline enthusiastically exclaimed, "and wait until you hear this! We took Mabel home and for a few days she kept pawing at the closet door in Mom's bedroom. Finally, I opened it and the puppy looked up to a shelf where Mom stored a knitting basket filled with Mabel's toys—you know, as keepsakes—and began wagging her little tail. I took the basket down, removed the old toys and replaced them with new ones I had just bought. We took the basket to the living room fully expecting Mabel to begin getting acquainted with them. She refused! Instead, she took them, one by one, walked back into Mom's bedroom and deposited each one in front of the closet door. We tried once more but got the same result.

"Finally, a few days later Mom said, 'Let's see what happens if we put a few of the old toys on the floor.' Sure enough, from a wide selection of about eight toys, the puppy picked up a stuffed duck that had been Mabel's favorite toy and ran around the living room with it in her mouth. I mean it was like she was saying to us, 'Now do you get it?' Mom fully accepted that her new puppy was really her beloved Mabel, reincarnated. I can't tell you what a restorative love she brought to Mom's life."

"Jacqueline," I said in a tone that indicated a slight shift in subject matter, "there's one more message to give your mother when you call her to tell her about our session. Your beloved father, Jonathan, is standing right here with us now, instructing me to tell you to tell your mom, 'Marjorie, my darling, tell Mabel welcome home for me, too. I'm so happy you finally let her back into your life, because she and I have been conspiring for her to return for nearly a year now.' "

At this writing, Marjorie and Mabel are thriving in their Hull, England, home, and Jacqueline is once again preparing for her annual visit.

WHOAHHH NELLIE!

Lucy was born to her parents late in life, so by the time she was in her late forties they had both passed over to their new dimension of living in the spirit world. Lucy inherited the Tennessee farm on which she was born, so she and her husband moved onto the property with their two sons, Levi and Jason. Years flew by and once the boys reached adulthood, she and her husband had an amicable divorce, after which Lucy decided she wanted to sell the farm and begin anew in a home of her own choosing. She requested a session with me to validate some guidance she had received from spirit, which is when she recounted the touching story of her journey with Nellie, her Shetland pony, and her dear parents.

Lucy's life as an only child on her parents' farm would have been quite lonely if it hadn't been for her beloved Shetland pony, Nellie, who faithfully followed her everywhere except inside the house and to school. Well, Nellie did accompany Lucy to school whenever her class was having "Pet Day," but otherwise she remained within the confines of the farm's corral.

Lucy described to me some of the games she and Nellie played together and hummed some of their favorite tunes. Being a highly sensitive little girl, Lucy was aware of subtle shifts in Nellie's expressions or when a song especially affected her. While she was in high school, Lucy entrusted Nellie with all the secrets a young girl might be tempted to share with her best friend—after all, with whom was Nellie going to gossip? With Nellie, Lucy was completely safe. By the time Lucy was ready for college, it was challenging to leave behind her beloved Nellie, her constant companion for eighteen years.

When Lucy came home for the holidays or during summer break, she and Nellie resumed their daily routine of mealtimes, walks, laying in the hay listening to music, and playing their favorite games. On this particular break, however, Lucy felt something different in Nellie that she couldn't quite pinpoint. While she was as affectionate and enthusiastic as ever, there was something subtle Lucy detected but did her best to convince herself was the result of still catching up on her rest after grueling finals at school. But a week later when she and her parents were driving into town to pick up feed for the animals and other errands, she finally decided to ask them if they had noticed anything different about Nellie.

Lucy's first clue that something was being withheld from her was her father, who, when she put the question to him, began biting his lower lip, something he did only when he was nervous. Turning to her mother, who was now shuffling through her purse looking for a shopping list, she asked, "Mom, is there something you're not telling me?"

"My mom said she'd prefer for the vet to explain the details to me," Lucy explained, "so that if I had any questions he could answer them. No matter how much I cajoled her, it became obvious I wasn't going to get anywhere. Three days later when we went to the vet he informed me Nellie had cancer and had about two to three months to live, which meant that by the time I would be coming home for Easter break she would most likely be gone.

"The day before I was leaving to head back to school, Nellie came up behind me, nudged me under the arm and positioned it around her neck. I knew right away that this was her way of saying goodbye. Less than three months later my mom called me at school to let me know that Nellie had crossed over, and that they buried her on the mound where she and I used to sit under a weeping willow tree watching the sunset."

Lucy then fast-forwarded to her decision to sell the house and what transpired upon hiring her real estate agent, Harriet.

"'I want to show you around a very special area,' Harriet told me, even though it was out of my price range. We had time to take a detour, so off we went. We'd packed a picnic lunch and found a lovely green field to spread out on. After a few minutes, I looked across the field and noticed a dust cloud heading our way. Then the dust cleared, and about twenty feet away I spotted a Shetland pony walking toward us. When it strolled to the low point of the corral over which we were sitting, the pony hung its head over the top of the wooden rail, reached over to where I was sitting, put its head under my arm, and lifted it up just as Nellie had done during our goodbye moment those many years ago. Then it began whinnying. And I matched its sounds with my crying.

"Harriet, having horses of her own, commented that this was an unusually friendly gesture for a horse's first contact with a new human being. But I was way ahead of her. The pony tugged not only at my arm but at my heartstrings and all the love I had for Nellie hit me like a thunderbolt."

She went on to describe that within minutes she and Harriet noticed a man running across the field, just not quite as fast as the horse had done and kicking up much less dust. Approaching the women he profusely apologized saying, "I hope this horse didn't scare you. We've had her for over a year. We bought her for our four-year-old son but no trainer has been able to calm her enough for my wife and I to feel Karl can handle her. We're just waiting for some repairs to be made to the barn and then we're going to sell . . ."

Lucy said she jumped to her feet and inquired about his sale price—both for the farm and the horse. The rest is what those feel-good movies that make us grab for Kleenex are made of! When Lucy shared with him a bit of her story, he not only ended up selling her the farm, he gave her the horse as a gift!

All of the details Lucy conveyed to me were for the purpose of validating what she intuitively felt was the spirit of Nellie reconnecting with her in a newly incarnated horse body. Was she misinterpreting or projecting her intuitive hit due to so passionately wanting it to be true—this was the burning question in her heart. Upon assuring her that her intuition was spot on, I was guided to provide the missing piece she wasn't quite prepared for.

"Lucy"—I began very slowly and soothingly—"you're not only right that your new horse is indeed Nellie reincarnated. There's more. Your dear parents are telling me they sent her to you. One of their deepest desires on the other side was to locate Nellie's spirit. By the time they were brought together—which needless to say is according to a different time measurement than we humans govern our lives by—Nellie was already preparing for her return. To use shamanic language, Nellie is your power animal, meant to walk alongside you throughout your lifetime as a loyal and loving companion from whom you can learn great wisdom and receive tremendous love."

"I've always believed in the synchronicity, but my consciousness has never expanded quite this far," Lucy tearfully shared.

Giving her some time to metabolize this new information, I asked, "Are you ready for more?"

"Oh my God," she exclaimed, "what's already been revealed is enough for a lifetime! Go ahead—let me have it," she said, pulling her shoulders back in a warrior's stance as though to say, "I can take anything."

"Your mother very thoughtfully wants me to tell you that it's time to begin preparing yourself for the wonderful life partner that you are going to meet through a synchronistic event in the near future. Knowing how sensitive you are, she thought it best for you to have advance notice, so she is really happy we're having this session today. And as you well know, your mom has a wicked sense of humor, so it will come as no surprise that she said she and your father have already had him fill out the application form and he passed with honors! Now she also added that while neither of you will find marriage necessary, you will live a beautiful, purposeful, and fulfilling life.

And so it came to pass that she met Gerard just as her mother had foretold, and to this day Nellie joins them on their daily walks, listening to music during barbecues on the patio, and taking naps together in the hay.

PEDRO THE DOUBLE YELLOW-HEADED AMAZON PARROT

Pedro was less than a year old when he was awarded the honorific title of "Parrot Prodigy" for his performance of opera. Admittedly, having been raised in a home where opera was the music of choice, Pedro had the advantage of getting an early start in his career. Although he had several operas in his repertoire and knew each one by name, his fans most frequently requested that he sing French composer Georges Bizet's opera *Carmen*.

The fact that Pedro was a street performer did not detract from his status in the least. In fact, taking a selfie with Pedro was such a popular draw to the eateries outside of which he performed that restaurateurs competed with one another for his presence because it drew customers to their respective doors.

Pedro's virtuoso was captivating in the video his owners, Juliette and Frank, played for me, not to mention the flair with which he swayed from side to side on his red wooden "stage" which was accented with black musical notes.

Although Pedro's wings had been clipped and he couldn't fly, he was able to glide around the interior of the house and land on perches they'd placed throughout—yes, they let him rule the kingdom so to speak—and from low tree branch to tree branch on the patio. At the age of five, Pedro somehow managed to glide as high as the ceiling fan in the living room and was instantly killed. How terribly Juliette and Frank suffered his loss and missed hearing him say "I am so handsome!"

Signs announcing Pedro's passing were posted outside of the restaurants where he performed, and many of his fans called his owners to express their condolences, some of whom had hired Pedro to sing at private events including birthday parties, weddings, pet shops, bird adoption shelters, to name a few. Many of them had not only photographed Pedro but also recorded him singing and speaking. How they missed him saying, "I love opera. Do you? I will sing for you!"

A couple of years had now gone by and, sadly, the couple had experienced another loss—Juliette's mother, Margaret, whom I also knew. When they made an appointment for a session to see how she was doing on the other side, Margaret wasted no time in saying, "Hans, please tell them Pedro is here and we're both doing very well. He sings to me and all those around us light up with radiant smiles. Let them know that

Pedro talks to them, too. Like this: 'Juliette, Frank, I'm still so handsome,' and then he breaks into song—*Carmen* of course. It's still his favorite."

I wasn't sure which of them touched Juliette and Frank more deeply—Margaret or Pedro! No doubt it was a tie, because all four of them were very close. The session ended so cheerfully, including a closing message from Margaret that they would have another bird in the near future. "Oh no," Juliette protested, "I don't think we could love another bird the way we did Pedro. He was our heart. Case closed!" She was right, at least for the time being.

About another year went by and I had flown to Los Angeles for a conference after which I'd arranged to meet Juliette and Frank for lunch in Sherman Oaks. After breaking bread together in a charming little restaurant, we were strolling down Ventura Boulevard to walk off the cheesecake we'd splurged on when an antiques store's window display caught our attention, drawing us inside the shop. While we walked around admiring its lovely vintage collection, in floated an aria from *Carmen*. "Where is that coming from?" Frank inquired. "It must be some record store or someone's car radio," Juliette responded.

When we crossed the street to continue burning off our calorie intake, it was a pet store that now attracted our attention because of a news truck for a broadcast television channel parked right outside its entrance. Curious, we went in to investigate. We elbowed our way through the crowd to the back of the store where a group was watching the filming. Frank's jaw dropped when the pet store owner announced to the interviewer, "This Double Yellow-headed Amazon parrot can sing." Turning to the parrot he said, "The stage is all yours!"

And that's when an aria from—you guessed it—*Carmen* froze us in place.

The interview concluded, the crowd dispersed, and as the store owners—an elderly couple—were shaking hands with the interviewer, Frank approached them with Juliette and me in tow.

"What a talented parrot! Did you teach him to sing opera?" he inquired, endeavoring to keep his emotions in check.

"You have no reason to believe us, but when we bought him as a very young bird he was old enough to sing, but where and how he learned opera is beyond us! We're country music fans and he did manage to pick up a couple of tunes. Even the breeder we bought him from had no explanation for his ability to sing opera. Anyway, his singing gained him notoriety so when the TV station wanted to feature him in an entertainment segment, they said we could let their audience know we were planning to retire, sell the store, and that Pedro was up for adoption."

"Did you just say Pedro?" Juliette said, sounding more accusatory than inquisitive.

"Yes, that was his name when we bought him. His breeder is from Mexico and all of his birds are given Spanish names," he patiently explained, "but of course anyone who buys the store or any of our birds before it sells can certainly change the names they've been given."

"Do you have any prospective buyers for the store?" Juliette inquired, after regaining her composure.

"Yes, as I was saying, we're hoping the TV shot will hurry up the sale because we've already purchased our retirement home in Arizona. Meanwhile, we're offering specials on all of our birds, fish, rabbits, reptiles, and of course our . . ."

Once again Juliette interrupted him and asked, "How much for Pedro?"

The wife spoke up saying, "I can't help saying that you seem to feel quite strongly about this bird."

Then she and Frank shared their experience about Pedro and his fondness for singing arias from *Carmen*, which he learned in their home since he was a baby. Stunned, the woman said, "I believe nothing happens by accident. You walked into our store at the perfect moment for you, your husband, and your Pedro. He's probably been waiting for just this day. Would you bless this Double Yellow-headed tenor by accepting him as a gift from us?"

I'm sure I don't have to tell you that this auspicious coming together concluded in tremendous joy for them and our "so handsome" winged friend, Pedro. To this day they still live in Sherman Oaks in a lovely home, one that has no ceiling fans.

I myself have had the blessing of having one of my beloved dogs return to me three times throughout this lifetime. And experience has taught me that even if a pet returns as a different species, they always give strong enough clues that make them absolutely recognizable to those with whom they have previously shared their lives. Over and over again it has been transmitted to me by an animal companion that he or she is returning to support a previous owner who is facing a life challenge and will be comforted and encouraged by their reunion. And the same is true for those who arrive in the spirit world and find themselves being greeted by a loving animal companion with whom they have shared their life. This, my friends, is the stunning grace that permeates our sacred interconnectedness, our unbroken kinship on every level of cosmic creation.

Notes

A Note to the Reader

1 Ervin Laszlo, *The Immortal Mind: Science and the Continuity of Consciousness beyond the Brain* (New York: Inner Traditions, 2014), 23.

Chapter 1: Heaven's Language

1 Dalai Lama, *Freedom in Exile: The Autobiography of The Dalai Lama* (San Francisco: HarperOne, 2008).

Chapter 2: Revelations of the Mystical Mirror

1 Mark Pendergrast, "A Conversation with Mark Pendergrast," accessed February 8, 2016. http://markpendergrast.com/mirror-conversation.

Chapter 3: The Anatomy of Spirit Guides

1. "Are Psychics for Real?" *Larry King Live*, CNN, airdate March 6, 2001.

Chapter 5: Spirit Guides: Ambassadors of Awakening

1 "The Shores of the Cosmic Ocean," *Cosmos: A Personal Voyage*, Episode 1, PBS, airdate September 28, 1980.
2 Deepak Chopra, *The Love Poems of Rumi* (New York: Harmony Books, 1998).
3 Paramahansa Yogananda, *Autobiography of a Yogi* (Los Angeles: Self-Realization Fellowship, 1998), 471.

Chapter 6: Karma and Dharma: Two Sides of the Cosmic Coin

1 Stanislav Grof, MD, *The Cosmic Game: Explorations of the Frontiers of Human Consciousness* (New York: State University of New York Press, 1998), 165–66.
2 Ian Stevenson, MD, *Where Reincarnation and Biology Intersect* (Westport, CT: Praeger, 1997), 5.
3 Carl G. Jung, *Memories, Dreams, Reflections* (New York: Vintage Books, 1965), 318.

Chapter 7: Velcro and Teflon Mind-sets: A Symbiotic Relationship

1 Chip Heath and Dan Heath, *Made to Stick: Why Some Ideas Survive and Others Die* (New York: Random House, 2007), 110–13.
2 Bruce Lipton, PhD, *The Wisdom of Your Cells* (Colorado: Sounds True, 2006). Audio CD.
3 Ibid.
4 Carl Sagan, *Cosmos* (New York: Random House, 1980), 339.
5 Ibid.

Chapter 8: Looking at Death with Seeing Eyes

1 Herman Feifel, ed., *The Meaning of Death* (New York: McGraw-Hill, 1959).

2 National Hospice and Palliative Care Organization, "History of Hospice Care," last modified July 23, 2015. accessed at http://www.nhpco .org/history-hospice-care.

3 Kathleen Dowling Singh, *The Grace in Dying: How We Are Transformed Spiritually as We Die* (New York: HarperOne, 1998), 7.

4 Kenneth Ring, "The Official Website of Dr. Kenneth Ring," accessed February 8, 2016. http://www.kenring.org/index.html.

Chapter 9: The Intuitive Intelligence of the Heart

1 Ray Kurzweil, *How to Create a Mind: The Secret of Human Thought Revealed* (New York: Viking Penguin, 2012).

2 Doc Lew Childre, Howard Martin, and Donna Beech, *The HeartMath Solution: The Institute of HeartMath's Revolutionary Program for Engaging the Power of the Heart's Intelligence* (New York: HarperCollins, 2000).

3 Michael A. Singer, *The Untethered Soul: The Journey Beyond Yourself* (Oakland, CA: New Harbinger Publications, 2007).

Chapter 11: Learning to Laugh Like a Buddha

1 Jane E. Brody, "Health: Personal Health," *New York Times*, April 7, 1988, accessed at http://www.nytimes.com/1988/04/07/us/health-personal-health.html.

2 Robert Provine, "The Science of Laughter," *Psychology Today* (November 1, 2000), accessed at https://www.psychologytoday.com/articles /200011/the-science-laughter.

3 Stephanie Eckelkamp, "Laughter Therapy Is the New Meditation," *Time*, May 2, 2014, accessed at http://time.com/84987/laughter-may-be-the-new-meditation/.

4 Kahlil Gibran, *Tears and Laughter* (New York: Philosophical Library, 1947).

5 Swami Beyondananda, "Swami's Daily Laughsitive," Wake Up Laughing, accessed February 2016 at http://wakeuplaughing.com/daily-laughsi tive.php.

Chapter 12: Love's Superpowers

1 Chopra, *The Love Poems of Rumi*, 19.
2 Paramahansa Yogananda, *The Bhagavad Gita* (Los Angeles: Self-Realization Fellowship, 1995).

Conclusion: You Are Your Own Religion

1 Eckhart Tolle, *A New Earth: Awakening to Your Life's Purpose* (New York: Penguin Group, 2005).
2 Hafiz, *The Gift* (New York: Penguin Compass, 1999).
3 Brian Swimme, *The Universe Is a Green Dragon: A Cosmic Creation Story* (Rochester, VT: Bear & Company, 1984).

Appendix B: Bonus Spirit Guide and Client Stories

1 J. Allen Boone, *Kinship with All Life* (New York: HarperCollins, 1954).

About the Author

Hans King was born in Los Angeles, California, the eldest of three children. At the tender age of three, he experienced one of the most defining moments of his life: He received his first visitation from his master guide, Sebastian. This otherworldly connection felt perfectly natural to Hans, as did that of his "guide tribe," who, under Sebastian's direction, prepared him for his unique calling as a direct-voice medium. Recognized as an internationally respected and sought after medium who has for fifty-five years served over fifty thousand clients, Hans is not only appreciated for his readings, but also for the profound spiritual insights he blends seamlessly into his sessions.

Deemed "one of the top five psychics in the country" by the *Miami Herald*, and by Brian Weiss, MD, as "a superb psychic and medium whose accuracy of 'hits' is impressive," in 2015 Shay Parker's Best American Psychics presented him with a Lifetime Achievement Award for his work in the field of metaphysics. Hans has shared his spiritual teachings through interviews on ABC and CBS television, NBC's *The Other Side*, and PBS's *Paranormal and Angels*. As well, he conducts teleseminars and facilitates an intensive series of Intuitive Development classes, which empower individuals to discover and activate their own innate clairsentience.

You may learn more about Hans King, his mediumship services, and classes by visiting: www.HansKing.com. Or call: 1-800-406-9027 for appointments and general information; international phone: + 1-828-258-1803.